Connected  Mathematics

Lesson Planner

D0128984

Prentice
Hall

Glenview, Illinois
Needham, Massachusetts
Upper Saddle River, New Jersey

The Connected Mathematics™ project was developed at Michigan State University with financial support from the Michigan State University Office of the Provost, Computing and Technology, and the College of Natural Science.

Connected Mathematics™ is based upon work supported by the National Science Foundation under Grant No. MDR 9150217.

Copyright © 2002 by Michigan State University, Glenda Lappan, James T. Fey, William M. Fitzgerald, Susan N. Friel, and Elizabeth D. Phillips. All rights reserved. Printed in the United States of America. This publication is protected by copyright, and permission should be obtained from the publisher prior to any prohibited reproduction, storage in a retrieval system, or transmission in any form or by any means, electronic, mechanical, photocopying, recording, or likewise. For information regarding permission(s), write to: Rights and Permissions Department.

ISBN 0-13-053139-1

6 7 8 9 10   05 04 03

Table of Contents

© Prentice-Hall, Inc.

Grade 7

© Prentice-Hall, Inc.

Grade 8

© Prentice-Hall, Inc.

Lesson Planner Introduction

This *Lesson Planner* is designed to help you plan more efficiently by providing a concise description of what is available and offering information about the mathematics related to the unit. It guides you to the many elements of *Connected Mathematics™*, including the Student Editions, Teacher's Guides, Teaching Resources (Assessment Masters, Transparencies, Blackline Masters and Additional Practice), and TestWorks™ CD-ROM with Assessment Resources and Additional Practice.

There are three parts to the Lesson Planner.
- **Unit Organizers**
- **Connections to Other Units**
- **Lesson Planners**

Unit Organizers

The Unit Organizers provide a one-page summary of the critical elements of each unit. The organizers include several parts.

Pacing Options offer estimates of class time needed for each Investigation and for assessment items. These charts are for more experienced CMP teachers. For teachers new to the curriculum, those who are teaching the unit for the first or second time, you may need to allow more time to cover the unit. The amount of, and need for, assessment will vary from site to site. You should choose the assessments and projects carefully.

Prerequisite Units are units that should be covered before attempting a particular unit. For some of the key mathematical ideas, the development occurs over several units within a grade level or across several units in one strand.

NCTM Principles and Standards 2000 advocates important areas of mathematics and mathematical thinking. This section shows how each unit of the CMP curriculum supports these standards.

Materials listed here are ones needed specifically for this unit. The list does not include items, such as rulers and scissors, that are assumed to be available in the typical classroom.

Teacher's Guide and Ancillary Resources indicate the availability of the TestWorks™ CD-ROM for Assessment and Additional Practice. This list also indicates the page numbers in the Teacher's Guide for locating the blackline masters of additional resource pages. These same resource materials are available separately as nine bound books: Assessment Resources (one for each of the three grade levels), Blackline Masters and Additional Practice (one for each of the three grade levels), and Transparencies (acetates, one set for each of the three grade levels).

Essential Vocabulary lists concepts that are essential for student understanding of this and future units. These words and concepts are deemed essential because of their usefulness in many mathematical situations.

Mathematics in the Unit lists the main objectives of the unit and, in doing so, summarizes much of the mathematics covered.

© Prentice-Hall, Inc.

Connections to Other Units

Most of the CMP units build on and connect to big ideas in other CMP units.
This page lists the following:

- the Big Ideas in a unit,
- previous CMP units where the mathematical foundations were developed, and
- still other units where these ideas will be extended later on.

Lesson Planners

One is provided for each investigation within the unit. The subparts of the planners are listed below.

Mathematical and Problem-Solving Goals are specific to the Investigation. The overall goal of *Connected Mathematics* is to help students develop sound mathematical habits.

Problems in this Investigation lists the titles of the problems and provides page numbers for easy location in the Student Edition.

Resource Options for Planning
Suggested Pacing
Assignment Guide
Materials for Students
Resources for Teachers

© Prentice-Hall, Inc.

Unit Organizer

Prime Time

Pacing Options

Investigations and Assessments	Class Time (days)
1 The Factor Game (SE, pp. 6–16)	3
2 The Product Game (SE, pp. 17–25)	5
3 Factor Pairs (SE, pp. 26–35)	4
Quiz A (TG, p. 69)	1
Check-Up 1 (TG, p. 68)	1/2
4 Common Factors and Multiples (SE, pp. 36–45)	3
5 Factorizations (SE, pp. 46–57)	4
Quiz B (TG, p. 71)	1
Check-Up 2 (TG, p. 70)	1/2
6 The Locker Problem (SE, pp. 58–64)	2
Looking Back and Looking Ahead: Unit Reflections (SE, pp. 66–67)	1
Self-Assessment (TG, p. 77)	take home
Unit Test (TG, p. 74)	1
Unit Project (SE, p. 65)	take home

Teacher's Guide and Ancillary Resources

Assessment Resources (pp. 67–93)

Blackline Masters (pp. 95–120)

Additional Practice (pp. 121–127)

 Assessment and Additional Practice

Essential Vocabulary

common factor	multiple
common multiple	odd number
composite number	prime factorization
even number	prime number
exponent	proper factor
factor	

Prerequisite Units

None

NCTM Principles and Standards 2000

Content Standard: Number and Operations

Process Standards: Problem Solving, Reasoning and Proof, Communication, Connections, and Representation

Materials

Calculators

Paper clips

Colored chips (about 12 each of 2 colors per pair)

Colored pens, pencils, or markers

Square tiles (about 30 per student)

Blank transparencies and transparency markers

12 signs with an open locker on one side and a closed door on the other (optional; provided as blackline masters)

Mathematics in the Unit

- Understand the relationships among factors, multiples, divisors, and products.
- Recognize that factors come in pairs.
- Link area and dimensions of rectangles with products and factors.
- Recognize numbers as prime or composite and as odd or even based on their factors.
- Use factors and multiples to explain some numerical factors of everday life.
- Develop strategies for finding factors and multiples of whole numbers.
- Recognize that a number can be written in exactly one way as a product of primes. (Fundamental Theorem of Arithmetic)
- Recognize situations in which problems can be solved by finding factors and multiples.
- Develop a variety of strategies — such as building a physical model, making a table or list, and solving a simpler problem — so solve problems involving factors and multiples.

© Prentice-Hall, Inc.

Connections to Other Units

The ideas in *Prime Time* build on and connect to several big ideas in other Connected Mathematics units.

Big Idea	Prior Work	Future Work
determining the factors of whole numbers; finding the greatest common factor of two numbers	learning and applying multiplication and division facts; applying the division algorithm *(elementary school)*	performing arithmetic operations with fractions *(Bits and Pieces I & II)*; comparing, scaling, and testing for similarity *(Stretching and Shrinking, Comparing and Scaling)*; factoring algebraic expressions *(Say It with Symbols)*
generating multiples of numbers; finding the least common multiple of two numbers	learning and applying multiplication facts; counting by 2s, 3s, etc. *(elementary school)*	understanding decimal numbers and the concept of place value *(Bits and Pieces I & II, Comparing and Scaling)*; identifying and analyzing patterns in the products of two numbers *(Covering and Surrounding, Variables and Patterns, Moving Straight Ahead, Say It with Symbols)*
determining factorizations, including the prime factorization, of a whole number	learning and applying multiplication and division facts; testing numbers for divisibility *(elementary school)*	finding the LCM in order to find common denominators for fractions and ratios *(Bits and Pieces I & II, Comparing and Scaling)*; studying patterns in multiplicative relationships to develop algorithms for finding area, surface area, and volume of figures *(Covering and Surrounding, Filling and Wrapping)*; identifying irrational numbers *(Looking for Pythagoras)*; studying exponential relationships *(Growing, Growing, Growing)*; developing and applying counting strategies *(Clever Counting)*
classifying numbers as prime or composite, as even or odd, and as abundant, deficient, or perfect	applying multiplication, addition, and division facts; comparing positive whole numbers *(elementary school)*	classifying numbers as positive or negative *(Accentuate the Negative)* and as rational or irrational *(Looking for Pythagoras)*; classifying relationships as linear, quadratic, or exponential *(Variables and Patterns; Moving Straight Ahead; Thinking with Mathematical Models; Growing, Growing, Growing; Frogs, Fleas, and Painted Cubes; Say It with Symbols)*

© Prentice-Hall, Inc.

Lesson Planner

Investigation 1: The Factor Game

Mathematical and Problem-Solving Goals

- To classify numbers as prime or composite
- To recognize that some numbers are rich in factors, while others have few factors
- To recognize that factors come in pairs and that once one factor is found, another can also be found
- To discover the connection between dividing and finding factors of a number

Problems in this Investigation

Problem 1.1: Playing the Factor Game *(pages 6–9)*

Problem 1.2: Playing to Win the Factor Game *(pages 10–11)*

Resource Options for Planning

	Suggested Pacing	Assignment Guide (ACE questions)	Materials for Students	Resources for Teachers
Investigation 1	3 days total	Exercises are in Student Edition, pp. 12–15	■ calculators ■ colored pens, pencils, or markers	■ Additional Practice, Investigation 1 (TG, p. 122)
Problem 1.1	1 day	1–9, 14	■ Labsheet 1.1 (1 per pair)	■ Transparency 1.1 (TG, p. 100) * ■ Labsheet 1.1 BLM (TG, p. 96)
Problem 1.2	2 days	10–13, 15–21	■ Labsheet 1.2 (1 per student)*	■ Transparency 1.2A (TG, p. 101) * ■ Transparency 1.2B (TG, p. 102) * ■ Labsheet 1.2 BLM (TG, p. 97)
Mathematical Reflections		MR 1–3	■ journal	

* optional materials

© Prentice-Hall, Inc.

Lesson Planner

Investigation 2: The Product Game

Mathematical and Problem-Solving Goals

- To review multiplication facts
- To develop understanding of factors and multiples and of the relationships between them
- To understand that some products are the result of more than one factor pair (for example, $18 = 9 \times 2$ and $18 = 6 \times 3$)
- To develop strategies for winning the Product Game
- To create a new Product Game to play with a friend

Problems in this Investigation

Problem 2.1: Playing the Product Game *(pages 17–18)*

Problem 2.2: Making Your Own Product Game *(page 19)*

Problem 2.3: Classifying Numbers *(pages 20–21)*

Resource Options for Planning

	Suggested Pacing (ACE questions)	Assignment Guide	Materials for Students	Resources for Teachers
Investigation 2	5 days total	Exercises are in Student Edition, pp. 22–24	■ calculators ■ blank transparency film and transparency markers *	■ Additional Practice, Investigation 2 (TG, p. 123)
Problem 2.1	1 day	1–8, 13, 17–20	■ Labsheet 2.1 (1 per pair) ■ paper clips (2 per pair) ■ colored chips (about 12 each of 2 colors per pair) ■ colored pens, pencils, or markers	■ Transparency 2.1 (TG, p. 103) * ■ Labsheet 2.1 BLM (TG, p. 98)
Problem 2.2	2 days	9, 10, 14	■ materials for constructing game boards (e.g., grid paper, construction paper, cardboard, markers) ■ paper clips ■ colored chips	■ Transparency 2.2 (TG, p. 104) *
Problem 2.3	2 days	11, 12, 15, 16		■ Transparency 2.3 (TG, p. 105) *
Mathematical Reflections		MR 1–3	■ journal	

* optional materials

© Prentice-Hall, Inc.

Investigation 3: Factor Pairs

Mathematical and Problem-Solving Goals

- To recognize that factors come in pairs
- To visualize and represent a factor pair as the dimensions of a rectangle with the given number as its area
- To determine whether a number is prime or composite, even or odd, and square or nonsquare based on its factor pairs
- To develop an informal sense of how many factors must be checked to be sure all the factors of a number have been found

Problems in this Investigation

Problem 3.1: Arranging Space *(pages 26–27)*

Problem 3.2: Finding Patterns *(pages 27–28)*

Problem 3.3: Reasoning with Odd and Even Numbers *(pages 28–29)*

Resource Options for Planning

	Suggested Pacing	Assignment Guide (ACE questions)	Materials for Students	Resources for Teachers
Investigation 3	4 days total	Exercises are in Student Edition, pp. 30–34	■ calculators ■ grid paper	■ Grid paper BLM (TG, p. 118) ■ Additional Practice, Investigation 3 (TG, p. 124)
Problem 3.1	1 day	16	■ square tiles (about 30 per pair)	■ Transparency 3.1 (TG, p. 106) *
Problem 3.2	1 day	1–8, 17–19, 21–25	■ blank sheets of paper ■ scissors ■ tape ■ square tiles (about 30 per pair) *	■ Transparency 3.2 (TG, p. 107) *
Problem 3.3 **Mathematical Reflections**	2 days	10–15 (26–30 as an extra challenge) MR 1–3	■ square tiles (about 30 per pair) * ■ journal	■ Transparency 3.3 (TG, p. 108) *

* optional materials

Investigation 4: Common Factors and Multiples

Mathematical and Problem-Solving Goals

■ To recognize situations in which finding factors and multiples of whole numbers will be helpful in answering questions

■ To observe and reason using patterns of factors and multiples

■ To use properties of factors and multiples to explain some numerical facts about everyday life

Problems in this Investigation

Problem 4.1: Riding Ferris Wheels *(pages 36–37)*

Problem 4.2: Looking at Locust Cycles *(page 38)*

Problem 4.3: Planning a Picnic *(page 39)*

Resource Options for Planning

	Suggested Pacing	Assignment Guide (ACE questions)	Materials for Students	Resources for Teachers
Investigation 4	3 days total	Exercises are in Student Edition, pp. 10–44	■ calculators	■ Additional Practice, Investigation 4 (TG, p. 125)
Problem 4.1	1 day	1–4		■ Transparency 4.1 (TG, p. 109) *
Problem 4.2	1 day	5–7, 14–16, 18		■ Transparency 4.2 (TG, p. 110) *
Problem 4.3	1 day	17, 21, 22 (19, 20, 23 as an extra challenge)		■ Transparency 4.3 (TG, p. 111) *
Mathematical Reflections		MR 1–4	■ journal	

* optional materials

© Prentice-Hall, Inc.

Investigation 5: Factorizations

Mathematical and Problem-Solving Goals

- To recognize that a number may have several different factorizations, but except for order, each number greater than 1 has exactly one factorization into a product of primes (the Fundamental Theorem of Arithmetic)

- To use several different strategies for finding the prime factorization of a number

- To recognize primes as the building blocks of whole numbers

Problems in this Investigation

Problem 5.1: Searching for Factor Strings *(pages 46–47)*

Problem 5.2: Finding the Longest Factor String *(pages 48–49)*

Problem 5.3: Using Prime Factorizations *(pages 50–51)*

Resource Options for Planning

	Suggested Pacing	Assignment Guide (ACE questions)	Materials for Students	Resources for Teachers
Investigation 5	4 days total	Exercises are in Student Edition, pp. 52–56	■ calculators	■ Additional Practice, Investigation 5 (TG, p. 126)
Problem 5.1	1 day	16, 17, 19	■ Labsheet 5.1 (1 per student)	■ Transparency 5.1 (TG, p. 112) * ■ Labsheet 5.1 BLM (TG, p. 99)
Problem 5.2	1 day	1–12, 21, 22		■ Transparency 5.2 (TG, p. 113) *
Problem 5.3	2 days	13–15, 20, 23, 24 (18 as an extra challenge)		■ Transparency 5.3 (TG, p. 114) *
Mathematical Reflections		MR 1–4	■ journal	

* optional materials

© Prentice-Hall, Inc.

Investigation 6: The Locker Problem

Mathematical and Problem-Solving Goals

■ To use ideas about the multiplicative structure of numbers—such as primes, composites, factors, multiples, and square numbers—to solve problems

■ To simulate a problem, gather data, make conjectures, and look for justification for those conjectures

■ To reason mathematically and to communicate ideas clearly

Problems in this Investigation

Problem 6.1: Unraveling the Locker Problem *(pages 58–60)*

Resource Options for Planning				
	Suggested Pacing	**Assignment Guide** (ACE questions)	**Materials for Students**	**Resources for Teachers**
Investigation 6	2 days total	Exercises are in Student Edition, pp. 61–63	■ calculators	■ Additional Practice, Investigation 6 (TG, p. 127)
Problem 6.1	2 days	1–7, 9, 10, 12, 14, 16		■ Transparency 6.1 (TG, p. 115) * ■ 12 signs denoting open and closed lockers (provided as BLM, TG, pp. 119–120) *
Mathematical Reflections		MR 1–4	■ journal	

* optional materials

© Prentice-Hall, Inc.

Data About Us

Pacing Options

Investigations and Assessments	Class Time (days)
1 Looking at Data (SE, pp. 6–21)	5
2 Types of Data (SE, pp. 22–29)	2
Check-Up (TG, p. 70)	1/2
3 Using Graphs to Group Data (SE, pp. 30–41)	2
4 Coordinate Graphs (SE, pp. 42–52)	2
5 What Do We Mean by *Mean*? (SE, pp. 53–67)	5
Looking Back and Looking Ahead: Unit Reflections (SE, pp. 69–70)	1
Quiz (TG, pp. 71–73)	1
Self-Assessment (TG, p. 80)	take home
Unit Test (TG, pp. 76–78)	1
Unit Project (SE, p. 68)	take home

Teacher's Guide and Ancillary Resources

Assessment Resources (pp. 69–92)

Blackline Masters (pp. 93–119)

Additional Practice (pp. 121–126)

 Assessment and Additional Practice

Essential Vocabulary

axis, axes

bar graph (bar chart)

categorical data

coordinate graph (scatter plot)

data	range
line plot	scale
mean	stem-and-leaf plot
median	(stem plot)
mode	survey
numerical data	table
outlier	

Prerequisite Units

Prime Time (Number and Operations)

NCTM Principles and Standards 2000

Content Standard: Data Analysis and Probability

Process Standards: Problem Solving, Reasoning and Proof, Communication, Connections, and Representation

Materials

Calculators

Index cards

Cubes (10 each of 6 different colors per student)

Stick-on notes

Colored pens, pencils, or markers

Large sheets of unlined paper

Yardsticks, metersticks, or tape measures

Mathematics in the Unit

- Engage in the process of data investigation: posing questions, collecting data, analyzing data, and making interpretations to answer questions.

- Represent data using line plots, bar graphs, stem-and-leaf plots, and coordinate graphs.

- Explore concepts that relate to ways of describing data, such as the shape of a distribution, what's typical in the data, measures of center (mode, median, mean), and range or variability in the data.

- Develop a variety of strategies—such as using comparative representations and concepts related to describing the shape of the data—for comparing data sets.

© Prentice-Hall, Inc.

Connections to Other Units

The ideas in *Data About Us* build on and connect to several big ideas in other Connected Mathematics units.

Big Idea	Prior Work	Future Work
collecting and organizing categorical and numerical data	analyzing and classifying integers *(Prime Time)*	gathering and organizing data collected from conducting experiments or trials of games *(How Likely Is It?, What Do You Expect?, Data Around Us, Samples and Populations)*
representing data with line plots, bar graphs, coordinate graphs, and stem-and-leaf plots	representing the number of proper factors of an integer *(Prime Time)*	representing data to aid with statistical analysis *(Data Around Us, Samples and Populations)*; expanding the use of coordinate grids to include negative coordinates *(Accentuate the Negative; Moving Straight Ahead; Thinking with Mathematical Models; Frogs, Fleas, and Painted Cubes; Say It With Symbols; Kaleidoscopes, Hubcaps, and Mirrors)*
finding measures of center	ordering numbers from smallest to largest, counting *(elementary school)*	using measures of center to make inferences and predictions about events or populations *(Data Around Us, Samples and Populations)*
finding measures of the "spread" of a set of data	comparing, counting, and ordering numbers *(elementary school)*	using the "spread" or "shape" of a data set to make judgments about the accuracy and reliability of the data and to make inferences and predictions about the group to which the data pertains *(Data Around Us, Samples and Populations)*
calculating the mean	using arithmetic operations (especially addition and division); learning the meaning of rational numbers (e.g., 2.5 is "between" the whole numbers 2 and 3) *(elementary school)*	developing further understanding about what the mean does and does not measure about a data set; using the mean together with other measures (e.g., median) to make predictions and inferences from data *(Data Around Us, Samples and Populations)*

© Prentice-Hall, Inc.

Lesson Planner

Investigation 1: Looking at Data

Mathematical and Problem-Solving Goals

- To use tables, line plots, and bar graphs to display data
- To use measures of center (mode and median) and measures of spread (range and intervals within the range) to describe what is typical about data
- To describe the shape of data
- To experiment with how the median, as a measure of center, responds to changes in the number and magnitude of data values

Problems in this Investigation

Problem 1.1: Organizing Your Data *(pages 6–7)*
Problem 1.2: Interpreting Graphs *(pages 7–9)*
Problem 1.3: Identifying the Mode and Range *(pages 9–10)*
Problem 1.4: Identifying the Median *(pages 11–13)*
Problem 1.5: Experimenting with the Median *(pages 13–14)*

Resource Options for Planning

	Suggested Pacing	Assignment Guide (ACE questions)	Materials for Students	Resources for Teachers
Investigation 1	5 days total	Exercises are in Student Edition, pp. 15–20	■ calculators	■ Additional Practice, Investigation 1 (TG, p. 122)
Problem 1.1	1 day	none		■ Transparency 1.1 (TG, p. 96) *
Problem 1.2	1 day	1		■ Transparency 1.2 (TG, p. 97) *
Problem 1.3	1 day	3–5, 7, 11–14	■ stick-on notes * ■ blank transparencies and transparency markers *	■ Transparency 1.3 (TG, p. 98) *
Problem 1.4	1 day	2, 6, 8, 9, 10	■ grid paper ■ scissors	■ Transparency 1.4A (TG p. 99) * ■ Transparency 1.4B (TG, p. 100) * ■ stick-on notes ■ chart paper with 1-inch grid *
Problem 1.5 **Mathematical Reflections**	1 day	Unassigned choices from earlier problems MR 1–7	■ index cards ■ journal	■ Transparency 1.5 (TG, p. 101) *

* optional materials

© Prentice-Hall, Inc.

Investigation 2: Types of Data

Mathematical and Problem-Solving Goals

■ To note the kind of data being collected; that is, categorical or numerical

■ To use bar graphs to display categorical and numerical data

■ To understand how measures of center (median and mode) and spread (range) relate to numerical and categorical data

Problems in this Investigation

Problem 2.1: Category and Number Questions *(pages 22–23)*

Problem 2.2: Counting Pets *(pages 23–25)*

Resource Options for Planning

	Suggested Pacing	Assignment Guide (ACE questions)	Materials for Students	Resources for Teachers
Investigation 2	2 days total	Exercises are in Student Edition, pp. 26–28	■ calculators	■ Additional Practice, Investigation 2 (TG, p. 123)
Problem 2.1	1 day	1–8	■ chart paper *	■ Transparency 2.1 (TG, p. 102) *
Problem 2.2	1 day	9–17		■ Transparency 2.2A (TG, p. 103) * ■ Transparency 2.2B (TG, p. 104) *
Mathematical Reflections		MR 1–3	■ journal	

* optional materials

© Prentice-Hall, Inc.

Lesson Planner

Investigation 3: Using Graphs to Group Data

Mathematical and Problem-Solving Goals

- To use stem-and-leaf plots to group numerical data in intervals
- To use the ordered data in a stem plot to locate measures of center (median and mode) and measure of spread (range)
- To describe the shape of the data, including the location of clusters and gaps, and to determine what is typical
- To compare two data sets by using back-to-back stem-and-leaf plots
- To compare two data sets by using statistics, such as median and range

Problems in this Investigation

Problem 3.1: Traveling to School *(pages 30–34)*

Problem 3.2: Jumping Rope *(pages 34–36)*

Resource Options for Planning

	Suggested Pacing	Assignment Guide (ACE questions)	Materials for Students	Resources for Teachers
Investigation 3	2 days total	Exercises are in Student Edition, pp. 37–40	■ calculators ■ graph paper	■ Additional Practice, Investigation 3 (TG, p. 124)
Problem 3.1	1 day	1–7		■ Transparency 3.1A (TG, p. 105) * ■ Transparency 3.1B (TG, p. 106) *
Problem 3.2	1 day	8, 9		■ Transparency 3.2 (TG, p. 107) * ■ local street map *
Mathematical Reflections		MR 1–3	■ journal	

* optional materials

© Prentice-Hall, Inc.

Lesson Planner

Investigation 4: Coordinate Graphs

Mathematical and Problem-Solving Goals

- To implement the process of statistical investigation to answer questions
- To review the process of measuring length, time, and distance
- To analyze data by using coordinate graphs to explore relationships among variables
- To explore intervals for scaling the vertical axis (y-axis) and the horizontal axis (x-axis)

Problems in this Investigation

Problem 4.1: Relating Height to Arm Span *(pages 42–44)*

Problem 4.2: Relating Travel Time to Distance *(pages 45–46)*

Resource Options for Planning

	Suggested Pacing	Assignment Guide (ACE questions)	Materials for Students	Resources for Teachers
Investigation 4	2 days total	Exercises are in Student Edition, pp. 47–51	■ calculators ■ grid paper	■ Additional Practice, Investigation 4 (TG, p. 125) ■ chart paper with 1-inch grid * ■ colored stick-on dots * ■ Grid paper BLM (TG, p. 119)
Problem 4.1	1 day	1–3	■ yardsticks, meter sticks, or tape measures ■ chart paper with 1-inch grid * ■ string	■ Transparency 4.1A (TG, p. 108) * ■ Transparency 4.1B (TG, p. 109) *
Problem 4.2	1 day	5	■ Labsheet 4.2 (1 per student) ■ Labsheet 4.ACE (1 per student)	■ Transparency 4.2 (TG, p. 110) * ■ Labsheet 4.2 BLM (TG, p. 92) ■ Labsheet 4.ACE BLM (TG, p. 93)
Mathematical Reflections		MR 1–4	■ journal	

* optional materials

© Prentice-Hall, Inc.

Lesson Planner

Investigation 5: What Do We Mean by *Mean*?

Mathematical and Problem-Solving Goals

- To understand the mean as a number that "evens out" or "balances" a distribution
- To create distributions with a designated mean
- To find the mean of a set of data
- To use the mean to help describe a set of data
- To reason with a model that clarifies the development of the algorithm for finding the mean
- To distinguish between the mean, median, and mode as ways to describe what is typical about a set of data

Problems in this Investigation

Problem 5.1: Evening Things Out *(pages 54–57)*

Problem 5.2: Finding the Mean *(page 57)*

Problem 5.3: Data with the Same Mean *(page 58)*

Problem 5.4: Using Your Class's Data *(page 59)*

Problem 5.5: Watching Movies *(pages 60–61)*

Resource Options for Planning

	Suggested Pacing	Assignment Guide (ACE questions)	Materials for Students	Resources for Teachers
Investigation 5	5 days total	Exercises are in Student Edition, pp. 62–66	■ calculators	■ Additional Practice, Investigation 5 (TG, p. 126)
Problem 5.1	1 day	1	■ cubes (10 each of 6 different colors per group)	■ Transparency 5.1A (TG, p. 111) * ■ Transparency 5.1B (TG, p. 112) * ■ cubes (10 each of 6 different colors) ■ stick-on notes *
Problem 5.2	1 day	2	■ cubes (10 each of 6 different colors per group) ■ stick-on notes ■ large sheets of unlined paper	■ Transparency 5.2 (TG, p. 113) *
Problem 5.3	1 day	3, 4	■ cubes (10 each of 6 different colors per group) ■ stick-on notes ■ large sheets of unlined paper	■ Transparency 5.3 (TG, p. 114) * ■ cubes (10 each of 6 different colors) ■ stick-on notes *
Problem 5.4	1 day	5–7	■ large sheets of unlined paper	■ Transparency 5.4 (TG, p. 115) *
Problem 5.5	1 day	8, 9		■ Transparency 5.5 (TG, p. 116) *
Mathematical Reflections		MR 1–4	■ journal	

* optional materials

© Prentice-Hall, Inc.

Unit Organizer

Shapes and Designs

Teacher's Guide and Ancillary Resources

Assessment Resources (pp. 77–97)

Blackline Masters (pp. 99–131)

Additional Practice (pp. 133–139)

 Assessment and Additional Practice

Essential Vocabulary

angle	rectangle
degree	regular polygon
hexagon	right angle
octagon	side
parallelogram	square
pentagon	symmetry
polygon	triangle
quadrilateral	vertex

Prerequisite Units

None

NCTM Principles and Standards 2000

Content Standard: Geometry, Measurement

Process Standards: Problem Solving, Reasoning and Proof, Communication, Connections, and Representation

Materials

Calculators

ShapeSet (1 per group)

Polystrips (1 per group)

Brass fasteners

Number cubes (3 per group; optional)

Angle rulers

Large sheets of unlines paper

Colored pens, pencils, or markers

ShapeSet for use on the overhead projector

Macintosh computer with Turtle Math software (optional)

Mathematics in the Unit

- Acquire knowledge of some important properties of polygons and a general ability to recognize those shapes and their properties.

- Describe decorative and structural applications in which polygons of various shapes appear.

- Hypothesize why hexagonal shapes appear on the surface of honeycombs.

- Explain the property of the triangle that makes it useful as a stable structure.

- Explain the side and angle relationships that make parallelograms useful for designs and for structures such as windows, doors, and tilings.

- Estimate the size of any angle using reference to a right angle and other benchmark angles.

- Use an angle ruler to make more accurate angle measurements.

- Develop a variety of strategies for solving problems involving polygons and their properties. Possible strategies include testing many different cases and looking for patterns in the results, finding extreme cases, and organizing results in a systematic way so that patterns are revealed.

© Prentice-Hall, Inc.

Connections to Other Units

The ideas in *Shapes and Designs* build on and connect to several big ideas in other Connected Mathematics units.

Big Idea	Prior Work	Future Work
understanding parts of polygons and how parts of polygons are related	developing mathematical reasoning by analyzing integers and data *(Prime Time, Data About Us)*; developing shape recognition skills *(elementary school)*	finding area and perimeter of 2-D figures *(Covering and Surrounding)*; studying properties of 3-D cube figures *(Ruins of Montarek)*; exploring similarity of 2-D figures *(Stretching and Shrinking)*; finding surface area and volume of 3-D figures *(Filling and Wrapping)*
learning important properties of polygons	developing classification skills through classifying integers (e.g., even, odd, abundant, deficient) and data (e.g., categorical or numerical) *(Prime Time, Data About Us)*; developing shape recognition skills *(elementary school)*	learning important properties of rectangles, triangles, and parallelograms *(Covering and Surrounding)*; studying properties of 3-D cube figures *(Ruins of Montarek)*; enlarging, shrinking, and distorting 2-D shapes *(Stretching and Shrinking)*; learning properties of 3-D figures *(Filling and Wrapping)*; learning and applying the Pythagorean Theorem *(Looking for Pythagoras)*
creating tilings with polygons and determining the properties of shapes that can be used to tile a surface	exploring how 2-D shapes fit together *(elementary school)*	understanding area as the exact number of square units needed to cover a 2-D figure *(Covering and Surrounding)*; subdividing figures into similar figures *(Stretching and Shrinking)*; connecting tessellations to isometries *(Kaleidoscopes, Hubcaps, and Mirrors)*
exploring symmetries in squares, rectangles, parallelograms, and equilateral triangles	exploring symmetry informally by looking at shapes of data sets *(Data Around Us)*	identifying symmetry in 3-D cubic figures *(Ruins of Montarek)*; connecting symmetry to isometries *(Kaleidoscopes, Hubcaps, and Mirrors)*
programming in Logo	exploring and playing with computer programs and computer games	continuing to program in Logo *(Covering and Surrounding; Stretching and Shrinking; Kaleidoscopes, Hubcaps, and Mirrors)*, working with graphing calculators *(Variables and Patterns; Moving Straight Ahead; Thinking with Mathematical Models; Frogs, Fleas, and Painted Cubes; Say It with Symbols)*

© Prentice-Hall, Inc.

Lesson Planner

Investigation 1: Bees and Polygons

Mathematical and Problem-Solving Goals

■ To discover, through exploration, which regular polygons can be used to tile a plane

■ To discover combinations of regular polygons that can be used to tile a plane

■ To discover that some irregular polygons can be used to tile a plane

Problems in this Investigation

Problem 1.1: Tiling a Beehive *(pages 8–10)*

Resource Options for Planning

	Suggested Pacing	Assignment Guide (ACE questions)	Materials for Students	Resources for Teachers
Investigation 1	2 days total	Exercises are in Student Edition, pp. 11–13	■ calculators	■ Additional Practice, Investigation 1 (TG, p. 134)
Problem 1.1	2 days	1–8, 12, 13	■ ShapeSet (1 per group)	■ Transparency 1.1 (TG, p. 106) * ■ ShapeSet for overhead projector ■ ShapeSet BLM (TG, pp. 129–130)
Mathematical Reflections		MR 1–2	■ journal	

* optional materials

© Prentice-Hall, Inc.

Lesson Planner

Investigation 2: Building Polygons

Mathematical and Problem-Solving Goals

■ To understand that triangles are stable figures that keep their shape under stress

■ To discover the triangle inequality—the sum of the lengths of any two sides of a triangle is greater than the length of the third side—through experimentation

■ To discover that quadrilaterals and other polygons are not stable shapes and become distorted under stress

■ To discover that the sum of the lengths of any three sides of a quadrilateral is greater than the length of the fourth side

Problems in this Investigation

Problem 2.1: Building Triangles *(page 16)*

Problem 2.2: Building Quadrilaterals *(page 17)*

Problem 2.3: Building Parallelograms *(page 18)*

Resource Options for Planning

	Suggested Pacing	Assignment Guide (ACE questions)	Materials for Students	Resources for Teachers
Investigation 2	3 days total	Exercises are in Student Edition, pp. 19–20	■ calculators ■ polystrips ■ brass fasteners	■ Additional Practice, Investigation 2 (TG, p. 135)
Problem 2.1	1 day	1, 2, 5, 7	■ large sheets of unlined paper for groups to record answers ■ number cubes (3 per group) *	■ Transparency 2.1 (TG, p. 107) *
Problem 2.2	1 day	3, 4, 6, 8, 14	■ large sheets of unlined paper for groups to record answers ■ number cubes (3 per group) * ■ isometric dot paper	■ Transparency 2.2 (TG, p. 108) * ■ isometric dot paper BLM (TG, p. 128)
Problem 2.3	1 day	Unassigned choices from previous problems		■ Transparency 2.3 (TG, p. 109) * ■ a few quadrilaterals cut out of paper (parallelograms, rectangles, and squares)
Mathematical Reflections		MR 1–4	■ journal	

* optional materials

© Prentice-Hall, Inc.

Lesson Planner

Investigation 3: Polygons and Angles

Mathematical and Problem-Solving Goals

- To develop an understanding of what an angle is and to find examples of angles in the real world
- To understand that the measure of an angle is the size of the opening or turn between its sides
- To learn that a full turn is divided into 360°, that half a turn measures 180°, and that a quarter turn measures 90°
- To estimate angle measures and to sketch angles using benchmarks
- To find precise angle measures using an angle ruler
- To use angles and angle meaures in real-life applications

Problems in this Investigation

Problem 3.1: Follow the Dancing Bee *(pages 22–25)*

Problem 3.2: Estimating Angle Measures *(pages 25–27)*

Problem 3.3: Developing More Angle Benchmarks *(pages 27–28)*

Problem 3.4: Playing Four in a Row *(pages 29–30)*

Problem 3.5 Using an Angle Ruler *(pages 30–31)*

Problem 3.6: Analyzing Measuring Errors *(pages 32–34)*

Resource Options for Planning

	Suggested Pacing	Assignment Guide (ACE questions)	Materials for Students	Resources for Teachers
Investigation 3	6 days total	Exercises are in Student Edltlon, pp. 35–40	■ calculators	■ Additional Practice, Investigation 3 (TG, p. 136)
Problem 3.1	1 day	Unassigned choices from previous problems		■ Transparency 3.1 (TG, p. 110) *
Problem 3.2	1 day	13–18, 27–29		■ Transparency 3.2A (TG, p. 111) * ■ Transparency 3.2B (TG, p. 112) * ■ Polystrips * ■ brass fasteners *
Problem 3.3	1 day	19–26 (estimates only)	■ ShapeSet (1 per group)	■ Transparency 3.3 (TG, p. 113) * ■ ShapeSet BLM (TG, pp.129–130)
Problem 3.4	1 day	43	■ Labsheet 3.4 (1 per student)	■ Transparency 3.4 (TG, p. 114) * ■ Labsheet 3.4 BLM (TG, p. 100)
Problem 3.5	1 day	1–12, 30–35, 38–42	■ Labsheet 3.5 (1 per student) ■ ShapeSet (1 per group) ■ angle rulers (1 per student)	■ Transparency 3.5 (TG, p. 115) * ■ transparency of Labsheet 3.5 ■ Labsheet 3.5 BLM (TG, p. 101) ■ ShapeSet BLM (TG, pp.129–130)
Problem 3.6 **Mathematical Reflections**	1 day	Unassigned choices from previous problems MR 1–5	■ Labsheet 3.6 (1 per student) ■ angle rulers ■ journal	■ Transparency 3.6 (TG, p. 116) * ■ Labsheet 3.6 BLM (TG, p. 102)

* optional materials

Shapes and Designs

© Prentice-Hall, Inc.

Lesson Planner

Investigation 4: Polygon Properties and Tiling

Mathematical and Problem-Solving Goals

- To use information about angles to test potential tiling problems
- To understand why and to show how any triangle can be used to tile
- To understand why squares, rectangles, parallelograms, and other quadrilaterals can be used to tile
- To show how regular hexagons can be used to tile
- To understand that most other polygons do not tile
- To understand that circular shapes do not tile

Problems in this Investigation

Problem 4.1: Relating Sides to Angles *(pages 42–44)*

Problem 4.2: Measuring Irregular Polygons *(pages 44–45)*

Problem 4.3: Back to the Bees! *(page 46)*

Resource Options for Planning

	Suggested Pacing	Assignment Guide (ACE questions)	Materials for Students	Resources for Teachers
Investigation 4	3 days total	Exercises are in Student Edition, pp. 47–49	■ calculators	■ Additional Practice, Investigation 4 (TG, p. 137)
Problem 4.1	1 day	1	■ angle rulers	■ Transparency 4.1 (TG, p. 120) *
Problem 4.2	1 day	2–6, 8, 10	■ Labsheet 4.2 * ■ straightedges ■ scissors	■ Transparency 4.2 (TG, p. 121) * ■ Labsheet 4.2 BLM (TG, p. 108) *
Problem 4.3	1 day	4	■ ShapeSet (1 per group)	■ Transparency 4.3 (TG, p. 122) * ■ ShapeSet for use on overhead projector
Mathematical Reflections		MR 1–2	■ journal	■ ShapeSet BLM (TG, pp. 129–130)

* optional materials

© Prentice-Hall, Inc.

Investigation 5: Side-Angle-Shape Connections

Mathematical and Problem-Solving Goals

- To recognize and describe flips and turns that will return a triangle, square, rectangle, or parallelogram to its original orientation

- To understand the properties of sides and angles in isosceles and equilateral triangles, squares, rectangles, and parallelograms

Problems in this Investigation

Problem 5.1: Flipping and Turning Triangles *(pages 52–53)*

Problem 5.2: Flipping and Turning Quadrilaterals *(pages 54–56)*

Resource Options for Planning

	Suggested Pacing	Assignment Guide (ACE questions)	Materials for Students	Resources for Teachers
Investigation 5	2 days total	Exercises are in Student Edition, pp. 57–62	■ calculators ■ ShapeSet (1 per group)	■ Additional Practice, Investigation 5 (TG, p. 138) ■ ShapeSet BLM (TG, pp. 129–130)
Problem 5.1	1 day	Unassigned choices from previous problems		■ Transparency 5.1 (TG, p. 124) *
Problem 5.2	1 day	1–17		■ Transparency 5.2 (TG, p. 125) *
Mathematical Reflections		MR 1–5	■ Journal	

* optional materials

© Prentice-Hall, Inc.

Lesson Planner

Investigation 6: Turtle Tracks

Mathematical and Problem-Solving Goals

- To use a computer programming language to reinforce ideas about the properties of polygons
- To lay a foundation for students to visualize exterior angles

Problems in this Investigation

Problem 6.1: Drawing with Logo *(pages 66–67)*

Problem 6.2: Debugging Computer Programs *(page 67)*

Problem 6.3: Making Polygons *(page 68)*

Resource Options for Planning

	Suggested Pacing	Assignment Guide (ACE questions)	Materials for Students	Resources for Teachers
Investigation 6	3 days total	Exercises are in Student Edition, pp. 69–74	■ calculators ■ Macintosh computers * ■ *Turtle Math* software * ■ grid paper *	■ Additional Practice, Investigation 6 (TG, p. 139) ■ grid paper BLM (TG, p. 127) *
Problem 6.1	1 day	1–8		■ Transparency 6.1 (TG, p. 122) *
Problem 6.2	1 day	5–11		■ Transparency 6.2 (TG, p. 123) *
Problem 6.3	1 day	18–25		■ Transparency 6.3 (TG, p. 124) *
Mathematical Reflections		MR A–D	■ journal	

* optional materials

© Prentice-Hall, Inc.

Unit Organizer

Bits and Pieces I

Pacing Options

Investigations and Assessments	Class Time (days)
1 Fund-Raising Fractions (SE, pp. 5–18)	5
2 Comparing Fractions (SE, pp. 19–30)	5
Check-Up 1 (TG, pp. 86–87)	1/2
3 Cooking with Fractions (SE, pp. 31–38)	2
Quiz (TG, pp. 88–89)	1
4 From Fractions to Decimals (SE, pp. 39–52)	4
5 Moving Between Fractions and Decimals (SE, pp. 53–66)	4
Check-Up 2 (TG, pp. 90–92)	1/2
6 Out of One Hundred (SE, pp. 67–83)	4
Looking Back and Looking Ahead: Unit Reflections (SE, pp. 84–86)	1
Self-Assessment (TG, p. 100)	take home
Unit Test (TG, pp. 96–98)	1

Teacher's Guide and Ancillary Resources

Assessment Resources (pp. 85–116)

Blackline Masters (pp. 117–172)

Additional Practice (pp. 173–179)

 Assessment and Additional Practice

Essential Vocabulary

decimal

denominator

equivalent fractions

fraction

numerator

percent

Prerequisite Units

Prime Time (Number and Operations)

NCTM Principles and Standards 2000

Content Standard: Number and Operations

Process Standards: Problem Solving, Reasoning and Proof, Communication, Connections, and Representation

Materials

Calculators

$8\frac{1}{2}$" strips of paper for making fraction strips

Distinguishing Digits Puzzle Cards (provided as BLM)

Square tiles (about 24 per student)

Colored cubes or tiles (optional)

Index cards (optional)

$8\frac{1}{2}$" fraction strips for the overhead projector

16 cm fraction strips for the overhead projector (optional; copy Labsheet 1.5 onto blank transparency film)

$5\frac{2}{3}$" strips of paper (optional)

A transparent centimeter ruler (optional)

Transparency of newspaper advertisement (optional)

Mathematics in the Unit

- Build an understanding of fractions, decimals, and percents and the relationships between and among these concepts and their representations.
- Develop ways to model situations involving fractions, decimals, and percents.
- Understand and use equivalent fractions to reason about situations.
- Compare and order fractions.
- Move flexibly between fraction, decimal, and percent representations.
- Use 0, $\frac{1}{2}$, 1, and $1\frac{1}{2}$ as benchmarks to help estimate the size of a number or sum.
- Develop and use benchmarks that relate different forms of representations of rational numbers (for example, 50% is the same as $\frac{1}{2}$ and 0.5).
- Use physical models and drawings to help reason about a situation.
- Look for patterns and describe how to continue the pattern.
- Use context to help reason about a situation.
- Use estimation to understand a situation.

© Prentice-Hall, Inc.

Connections to Other Units

The ideas in *Shapes and Designs* build on and connect to several big ideas in other Connected Mathematics units.

Big Idea	Prior Work	Future Work
understanding, comparing, and applying fractions	comparing whole numbers and finding least common multiples *(Prime Time)*; studying 2-D shapes to understand better their use as area models *(Shapes and Designs)*	developing algorithms for performing calculations *(Bits and Pieces II)*; using scale factors *(Stretching and Shrinking)*; applying rational numbers *(Comparing and Scaling)*; interpreting slope *(Moving Straight Ahead)*; interpreting fractions as probabilities *(What Do You Expect?)*; identifying and finding equivalent expressions *(Say It With Symbols)*
understanding, comparing, and applying decimals	comparing whole numbers; exploring multiples of 10 *(Prime Time)*; studying 2-D shapes to understand better their use as area models *(Shapes and Designs)*	interpreting decimals as probabilities *(How Likely Is It?, What Do You Expect?)*; applying rational numbers *(Bits and Pieces II, Comparing and Scaling, Samples and Populations)*
understanding, comparing, and applying percents	comparing whole numbers; finding the greatest common factor or least common multiple of two numbers *(Prime Time)*; using area models to better understand percent as a comparison to 100 *(Shapes and Designs)*	applying rational numbers *(Bits and Pieces II, Comparing and Scaling, Samples and Populations)*; interpreting percents as probabilities *(How Likely Is It?, What Do You Expect?)*; working with statistics and data reported as percents *(Data Around Us)*
connecting fractions, decimals, and percents	studying multiples and exponents *(Prime Time)*; studying 2-D shapes to better compare area models of fractions, decimals, and percents *(Shapes and Designs)*; dividing whole numbers *(elementary school)*	using fractions, decimals, and percents as expressions of probabilities *(How Likely Is It?, What Do You Expect?, Samples and Populations)*; using fractions and decimals as slopes or variable coefficients in equations *(Variables and Patterns; Moving Straight Ahead; Thinking with Mathematical Models; Growing, Growing, Growing; Frogs, Fleas, and Painted Cubes; Say It With Symbols)*; connecting fractions, decimals, and percents by interpreting percentages and decimals as fractions *(Bits and Pieces II, Comparing and Scaling)*

© Prentice-Hall, Inc.

Lesson Planner

Investigation 1: Fund-Raising Fractions

Mathematical and Problem-Solving Goals

■ To use the part-whole interpretation of fractions to create a set of fraction strips

■ To relate the fraction-strip model to the part-whole interpretation of fractions and to the symbolic representation of fractions

■ To understand the meaning of fractions larger than a whole

■ To use fraction strips and symbolic representations of fractions to describe real-world situations

Problems in this Investigation

Problem 1.1: Reporting our Progress *(page 5)*

Problem 1.2: Using Fraction Strips *(pages 6–7)*

Problem 1.3: Comparing Classes *(pages 8–9)*

Problem 1.4: Exceeding the Goal *(pages 10–11)*

Problem 1.5: Using Symbolic Form *(pages 12–13)*

Resource Options for Planning

	Suggested Pacing	Assignment Guide (ACE questions)	Materials for Students	Resources for Teachers
Investigation 1	5 days total	Exercises are in Student Edition, pp. 14—17	■ calculators	■ Additional Practice, Investigation 1 (TG, p. 174)
Problem 1.1	1 day	see TG p. 5		■ Transparency 1.1 (TG, p. 128) *
Problem 1.2	1 day	26	■ $8\frac{1}{2}$" strips of paper (9 per student)	■ Transparency 1.2A (TG, p. 129) * ■ Transparency 1.2B (TG, p. 130) * ■ $8\frac{1}{2}$" fraction strips for the overhead projector
Problem 1.3	1 day	13–25	■ $8\frac{1}{2}$" strips of paper (9 per student)	■ Transparency 1.3A (TG, p. 131) * ■ Transparency 1.3B (TG, p. 132) * ■ $8\frac{1}{2}$" fraction strips for the overhead projector
Problem 1.4	1 day	8–11		■ Transparency 1.4A (TG, p. 133) * ■ Transparency 1.4B (TG, p. 134) * ■ $8\frac{1}{2}$" fraction strips for the overhead projector
Problem 1.5	1 day	1–7, 12	■ Labsheet 1.5 (1 per student)	■ Transparency 1.5 (TG, p. 135) * ■ $8\frac{1}{2}$" fraction strips for the overhead projector ■ transparent centimeter ruler * ■ 16 cm fraction strips for the overhead projector (Labsheet 1.5, TG p. 118)
Mathematical Reflections		MR 1–3	■ journal	

* optional materials

© Prentice-Hall, Inc.

Lesson Planner

Investigation 2: Comparing Fractions

Mathematical and Problem-Solving Goals

■ To continue to use fraction strips as tools for understanding fraction concepts

■ To investigate the concepts of comparison and equivalence of fractions

■ To use fractions that are less than, equal to, and greater than 1

■ To apply knowledge gained by using fraction strips to name, estimate, and compare fractions and to find equivalent fractions

■ To build a number line and label points between whole numbers

Problems in this Investigation

Problem 2.1: Comparing Notes *(page 19)*

Problem 2.2: Finding Equivalent Fractions *(pages 20–21)*

Problem 2.3: Making a Number Line *(pages 22–23)*

Problem 2.4: Comparing Fractions to Benchmarks *(pages 23–24)*

Problem 2.5: Fractions Greater Than One *(pages 24–25)*

Resource Options for Planning

	Suggested Pacing	Assignment Guide (ACE questions)	Materials for Students	Resources for Teachers
Investigation 2	5 days total	Exercises are in Student Edition, pp. 21–26	■ calculators	■ Additional Practice, Investigation 2 (TG, p. 175) ■ fraction strips for the overhead projector (Labsheet 1.5)
Problem 2.1	1 day	Unassigned choices from earlier problems		■ Transparency 2.1 (TG, p. 136) *
Problem 2.2	1 day	1–7, 19, 38–40		■ Transparency 2.2A (TG, p. 137) * ■ Transparency 2.2B (TG, p. 138) *
Problem 2.3	1 day	20–27, 37	■ labeled fraction strips from Labsheet 1.5	■ Transparency 2.3 (TG, p. 139) *
Problem 2.4	1 day	8–15, 41, 42		■ Transparency 2.4 (TG, p. 140) * ■ index cards *
Problem 2.5	1 day	16–18, 28–36	■ labeled fraction strips from Labsheet 1.5	■ Transparency 2.5 (TG, p. 141) * ■ large number line to display in the classroom
Mathematical Reflections		MR 1–3	■ journal	

* optional materials

© Prentice-Hall, Inc.

Investigation 3: Cooking with Fractions

Mathematical and Problem-Solving Goals

- To continue building an understanding of equivalent fractions
- To explore the use of squares and other areas as a way to build visual models of fractional parts of a whole
- To explore real-life problems that require operations on fractions in a context that invites the use of informal strategies rather than formal rules and algorithms

Problems in this Investigation

Problem 3.1: Area Models for Fractions *(pages 31–32)*
Problem 3.2: Baking Brownies *(pages 32–33)*

Resource Options for Planning

	Suggested Pacing	Assignment Guide (ACE questions)	Materials for Students	Resources for Teachers
Investigation 3	2 days total	Exercises are in Student Edition pp. 34–37	■ calculators	■ Additional Practice, Investigation 3 (TG, p. 176)
Problem 3.1	1 day	13, 18–23, 24–32	■ Labsheet 3.1 (1 per student)	■ Transparency 3.1 (TG, p. 142) * ■ Labsheet 3.1 BLM (TG p. 119)
Problem 3.2	1 day	14–17	■ rulers or other straightedges	■ Transparency 3.2A (TG, p. 143) * ■ Transparency 3.2B (TG, p. 144) *
Mathematical Reflections		MR 1–3	■ journal	

* optional materials

© Prentice-Hall, Inc.

Lesson Planner

Investigation 4: From Fractions to Decimals

Mathematical and Problem-Solving Goals

- To extend knowledge of place value of whole numbers to decimal numbers
- To represent fractions with denominators of 10 and powers of 10 as decimal numbers
- To visualize the representation of decimal numbers using a 10-by-10-grid area model
- To relate fraction benchmarks to decimal benchmarks
- To write, compare, and order decimals with place values to ten-thousandths

Problems in this Investigation

Problem 4.1: Designing a Garden *(pages 39–40)*

Problem 4.2: Making Smaller Parts *(pages 41–43)*

Problem 4.3: Using Decimal Benchmarks *(pages 43–44)*

Problem 4.4: Playing Distinguishing Digits *(page 45)*

Resource Options for Planning

	Suggested Pacing	Assignment Guide (ACE questions)	Materials for Students	Resources for Teachers
Investigation 4	4 days total	Exercises are in Student Edition, pp. 38–44	■ calculators ■ grid paper	■ Additional Practice, Investigation 4 (TG, p. 177) ■ grid paper BLM (TG p. 172)
Problem 4.1	1 day	38–41	■ Labsheet 4.1 (1 per student) ■ colored cubes or tiles (100 per group) * ■ Transparency 4.2D and transparency markers *	■ Transparency 4.1 (TG, p. 145) * ■ Labsheet 4.1 BLM (TG, p. 120)
Problem 4.2	1 day	1–9	■ Labsheet 4.2 (1 per student) ■ Labsheet 4.ACE (1 per student)	■ Transparency 4.2A (TG, p. 146) * ■ Transparency 4.2B (TG, p. 147) * ■ Transparency 4.2C (TG, p. 148) * ■ Transparency 4.2D (TG, p. 149) * ■ Transparency 4.2E (TG, p. 150) * ■ Transparency 4.2F (TG, p. 151) * ■ Transparency 4.2G (TG, p. 152) * ■ Labsheet 4.2 BLM (TG, p. 121) ■ Labsheet 4.ACE BLM (TG, p. 122)
Problem 4.3	1 day	10–36, 43, 44	■ Distinguishing Digits cards	■ Transparency 4.3 (TG, p. 153) * ■ Distinguishing Digits cards BLM (TG, pp. 166–171)
Problem 4.4	1 day	Unassigned choices from earlier problems		■ Transparency 4.4 (TG, p. 154)*
Mathematical		MR 1–4	■ journal	

* optional materials

© Prentice-Hall, Inc.

Investigation 5: Moving Between Fractions and Decimals

Mathematical and Problem-Solving Goals

- To understand that the decimal representation of a fraction shows the same proportion but is based on a power of 10 as the denominator
- To use the concept of equivalence to change the form of simple fractions to fractions with 100 in the denominator
- To understand the division interpretation of fractions and use it to change fractions to decimals
- To use fraction strips to estimate fractions as decimals and decimals as fractions
- To find equivalent forms of fraction quantities
- To use hundredths grids to model fractions
- To use knowledge of operations, fractions, and decimals to understand real-world situations

Problems in this Investigation

Problem 5.1: Choosing the Best *(pages 53–54)*

Problem 5.2: Writing Fractions as Decimals *(pages 54–56)*

Problem 5.3: Moving From Fractions to Decimals *(page 57)*

Resource Options for Planning

	Suggested Pacing	Assignment Guide (ACE questions)	Materials for Students	Resources for Teachers
Investigation 5	4 days total	Exercises are in Student Edition, pp. 58–65	■ calculators	■ Additional Practice, Investigation 5 (TG, p. 178) ■ transparency of centimeter grid paper *
Problem 5.1	1 day	17–24, 39	■ Labsheet 5.1 (1 per student) ■ colored tiles*	■ Transparency 5.1 (TG, p. 155) * ■ Labsheet 5.1 BLM (TG p. 117)
Problem 5.2	1 day	1–16, 35–38	■ Labsheet 5.2 (1 per student) ■ straightedges ■ chart paper or a transparency of Labsheet 5.2 and transparency markers *	■ Transparency 5.2 (TG, p. 156) * ■ Transparency 4.2D
Problem 5.3 **Mathematical Reflections**	2 days	25–31, 33, 34, 40–50 MR 1–3	■ Labsheet 5.2 ■ journal	■ Transparency 5.3 (TG, p. 157) *

* optional materials

© Prentice-Hall, Inc.

Lesson Planner

Investigation 6: Out of One Hundred

Mathematical and Problem-Solving Goals

- To use the "out of 100" interpretations of fractions and decimals to develop an understanding of percent

- To use the hundredths grid to visualize the concept of percent as meaning "out of 100"

- To investigate the relationships among fractions, decimals, and percents and to move flexibly among representations

- To understand how to use percent as an expression of frequency, in terms of "out of 100," when a set of data has more or fewer than 100 items

Problems in this Investigation

Problem 6.1: It's Raining Cats *(pages 68–73)*

Problem 6.2: Dealing with Discounts *(pages 73–75)*

Problem 6.3: Changing Forms *(page 75)*

Problem 6.4: It's Raining Cats and Dogs *(page 76)*

Resource Options for Planning

	Suggested Pacing	Assignment Guide (ACE questions)	Materials for Students	Resources for Teachers
Investigation 6	4 days total	Exercises are in Student Edition, pp. 77–82	■ calculators	■ Additional Practice, Investigation 6 (TG, p. 179)
Problem 6.1	1 day	1–8, 12	■ Labsheet 6.1	■ Transparency 6.1A (TG, p. 158) * ■ Transparency 6.1B (TG, p. 159) * ■ Labsheet 6.1 BLM (TG, p. 125)
Problem 6.2	1 day	9–11, 14–15	■ hundredths strips (from Labsheet 5.2) ■ fraction strips * ■ hundredths grids (from Labsheet 5.1)	■ Transparency 6.2 (TG, p. 160) * ■ Labsheet 5.2 BLM (TG, p. 124) ■ Labsheet 5.1 BLM (TG, p. 123) ■ transparency of newspaper advertisements *
Problem 6.3	1 day	13, 17–20, 22–28	■ Labsheet 6.3 ■ hundredths strips (from Labsheet 5.2) ■ Labsheet 6.ACE	■ Transparency 6.3 (TG, p. 161) * ■ Labsheet 6.3 BLM (TG, p. 126) ■ Labsheet 5.2 BLM (TG, p. 124) ■ Labsheet 6.ACE BLM (TG, p. 127)
Problem 6.4	1 day	21	■ hundredths grids (from Labsheet 5.1)	■ Transparency 6.4A (TG, p. 162) * ■ Transparency 6.4B (TG, p. 163) * ■ Labsheet 5.1 BLM (TG, p. 123)
Mathematical Reflections		MR 1–5	■ journal	

* optional materials

© Prentice-Hall, Inc.

Covering and Surrounding

Pacing Options

Investigations and Assessments	Class Time (days)
1 Measuring Perimeter and Area (SE, pp. 6–18)	4
2 Measuring Odd Shapes (SE, pp. 19–28)	2
3 Constant Area, Changing Perimeter (SE, pp. 29–34)	2
4 Constant Perimeter, Changing Area (SE, pp. 35–45)	2
Check-Up 1 (TG, p. 86)	1/2
Quiz A (TG, pp. 87–88)	1
5 Measuring Parallelograms (SE, pp. 46–55)	3
6 Measuring Triangles (SE, pp. 56–68)	4
7 Going Around in Circles (SE, pp. 69–81)	6
Looking Back and Looking Ahead: Unit Reflections (SE, pp. 84–86)	1
Check-Up 2 (TG, pp. 89–90)	1/2
Quiz B (TG, pp. 91–92)	1
Self-Assessment (TG, p. 101)	take home
Unit Test (TG, pp. 98–99)	1
Unit Project (SE, pp. 82–83)	take home

Teacher's Guide and Ancillary Resources

Assessment Resources (pp. 85–114)

Blackline Masters (pp. 115–148)

Additional Practice (pp. 149–156)

 Assessment and Additional Practice

Essential Vocabulary

area

center (of a circle)

circle

circumference

diameter

perimeter

radius (radii)

pi or π

Prerequisite Units

Prime Time (Number and Operations)

Shapes and Designs (Geometry and Measurement)

Bits and Pieces I (Number and Operations)

NCTM Principles and Standards 2000

Content Standard: Measurement

Process Standards: Problem Solving, Reasoning and Proof, Communication, Connections, and Representation

Materials

Square tiles (about 24 per student)

Compasses

String

Several circular objects

Transparencies and markers

Grid paper

Mathematics in the Unit

- Develop strategies for finding areas and perimeters of rectangular shapes and of nonrectangular shapes.
- Discover relationships between perimeter and area.
- Understand how the area of a rectangle is related to the area of a triangle and of a parallelogram.
- Develop formulas or procedures—stated in words or symbols—for finding areas and perimeters of rectangles, parallelograms, triangles, and circles.
- Use area and perimeter to solve applied problems.
- Recognize situations in which measuring perimeter or area will answer practical problems.
- Find perimeters and areas of rectangular and nonrectangular figures by using transparent grids, tiles, or other objects to cover the figures and string, straight-line segments, rulers, or other objects to surround the figures.
- Cut and rearrange figures—in particular, parallelograms, triangles, and rectangles—to see relationships between them and then devise strategies for finding areas by using the observed relationships.
- Observe and reason from patterns in data by organizing tables to represent the data.
- Reason to find, confirm, and use relationships involving area and perimeter.
- Use multiple representations—in particular, physical, pictoral, tabular, and symbolic models—and verbal descriptions of data.

© Prentice-Hall, Inc.

Connections to Other Units

The ideas in *Covering and Surrounding* build on and connect to several big ideas in other Connected Mathematics units.

Big Idea	Prior Work	Future Work
interpreting area as the number of square units needed to cover a 2-D shape	creating tessellations *(Shapes and Designs)*	studying relationships between 3-D models and 2-D representations of the models *(Ruins of Montarek)*; comparing areas of 2-D shapes to test for similarity *(Stretching and Shrinking)*; finding surface area and volume of 3-D figures *(Filling and Wrapping)*
interpreting perimeter as the number of (linear) units needed to surround a 2-D shape	using Logo to construct shapes with the computer *(Shapes and Designs)*	studying relationships between 3-D models and 2-D representations of the models *(Ruins of Montarek)*; looking at dimensions of similar figures to find scale factors *(Stretching and Shrinking)*; finding surface area and volume of 3-D figures *(Filling and Wrapping)*
developing strategies for finding the perimeter and area of irregular 2-D shapes	performing operations with rational numbers; estimating sums of rational numbers *(Prime Time, Bits and Pieces I)*	developing strategies for estimating the surface area and volume of irregular 3-D figures *(Filling and Wrapping)*
studying the relationship between perimeter and area in rectangles	performing operations with whole numbers and finding factor pairs of whole numbers *(Prime Time)*; using and constructing graphs on coordinate grids *(Data About Us)*	studying the relationship between the dimensions and volume of a prism *(Filling and Wrapping)*
developing strategies and algorithms for finding the perimeter and area of rectangles, triangles, parallelograms, and circles	subdividing and comparing shapes *(Shapes and Designs)*; collecting data and looking for and generalizing patterns *(Prime Time, Shapes and Designs*	developing strategies and algorithms for finding the surface area and volume of prisms, cones, and spheres *(Filling and Wrapping)*

© Prentice-Hall, Inc.

Lesson Planner

Investigation 1: Measuring Perimeter and Area

Mathematical and Problem-Solving Goals

■ To learn that the area of an object is the number of unit squares needed to cover it and the perimeter of an object is the number of units of length needed to surround it

■ To understand that two figures with the same area may have different perimeters and that two figures with the same perimeter may have different areas

■ To visualize what changes occur when tiles forming a figure are rearranged, added, or subtracted

Problems in this Investigation

Problem 1.1: Designing Bumper-Car Rides *(pages 6–7)*

Problem 1.2: Decoding Designs *(pages 8–9)*

Problem 1.3: Computing Costs *(pages 10–11)*

Problem 1.4: Getting Your Money's Worth *(page 11)*

Resource Options for Planning

	Suggested Pacing	Assignment Guide (ACE questions)	Materials for Students	Resources for Teachers
Investigation 1	4 days total	Exercises are in Student Edition, pp. 13–17	■ calculators ■ centimeter grid paper	■ Additional Practice, Investigation 1 (TG, p. 150) ■ Centimeter grid paper BLM (TG, p. 145)
Problem 1.1	1 day	see TG p. 6	■ square tiles (24 per student)	■ Transparency 1.1 (TG, p. 120) * ■ square tiles
Problem 1.2	1 day	1, 6–9	■ inch grid paper or one-inch tiles	■ Transparency 1.2A (TG, p. 121) * ■ Transparency 1.2B (TG, p. 122) * ■ Inch grid paper or one-inch tiles BLM (TG, p. 148)
Problem 1.3	1 day	Unassigned choices from earlier problems		■ Transparency 1.3A (TG, p. 123) * ■ Transparency 1.3B (TG, p. 124) *
Problem 1.4 **Mathematical Reflections**	1 day	2–5, 10, 11, 14–18 MR 1–3	■ square tiles (24 per student) ■ grid paper ■ journal	■ Transparency 1.4 (TG, p. 125) ■ blank transparencies *

* optional materials

© Prentice-Hall, Inc.

Lesson Planner

Investigation 2: Measuring Odd Shapes

Mathematical and Problem-Solving Goals

- To understand the meaning of area and perimeter
- To develop techniques for estimating areas and perimeters of nongeometric figures
- To develop strategies for organizing and comparing data
- To use graphs to organize data and to make predictions

Problems in this Investigation

Problem 2.1: Making the Shoe Fit *(pages 19–20)*

Resource Options for Planning

	Suggested Pacing	Assignment Guide (ACE questions)	Materials for Students	Resources for Teachers
Investigation 2	2 days total	Exercises are in Student Edition, pp. 21–26	■ calculators ■ string ■ centimeter rulers ■ centimeter grid paper	■ Additional Practice, Investigation 2 (TG, p. 151) ■ Centimeter grid paper BLM (TG, p. 145)
Problem 2.1	2 days	1–24	■ city or state map ■ world atlas or encyclopedia ■ transparencies of centimeter grid paper	■ Transparency 2.1 (TG, p. 126) *
Mathematical Reflections		MR 1–3	■ journal	

* optional materials

© Prentice-Hall, Inc.

Investigation 3: Constant Area, Changing Perimeter

Mathematical and Problem-Solving Goals

- To understand how the perimeters of rectangles can vary considerably even when the area is held constant

- To construct diagrams and tables to organize and represent data

- To explore maxima/minima questions in the context of finding the largest and smallest perimeters for rectangles of a fixed area

- To continue to develop a conceptual understanding of area and perimeter

Problems in this Investigation

Problem 3.1: Building Storm Shelters *(pages 29–30)*

Problem 3.2: Stretching the Perimeter *(pages 30–31)*

Resource Options for Planning

	Suggested Pacing	Assignment Guide (ACE questions)	Materials for Students	Resources for Teachers
Investigation 3	2 days total	Exercises are in Student Edition, pp. 24–27	■ calculators ■ centimeter grid paper	■ Additional Practice, Investigation 3 (TG, p. 152) ■ Centimeter grid paper BLM (TG, p. 145)
Problem 3.1	1 day	1–6	■ square tiles (24 per student)	■ Transparency 3.1 (TG, p. 127) *
Problem 3.2	1 day	7, 8	■ string ■ scissors	■ Transparency 3.2 (TG, p. 128) * ■ 4x6 rectangle cut from inch grid paper
Mathematical Reflections		MR 1–3	■ journal	

* optional materials

© Prentice-Hall, Inc.

Investigation 4: Constant Perimeter, Changing Area

Mathematical and Problem-Solving Goals

- To learn that the areas of rectangles with a fixed perimeter can vary considerably
- To construct diagrams and tables to organize and represent data
- To find the minimum and maximum areas of rectangles with a fixed perimeter
- To distinguish the case of fixed area from the case of fixed perimeter
- To continue to develop a conceptual understanding of area and perimeter

Problems in this Investigation

Problem 4.1: Fencing in Spaces *(pages 35–36)*

Problem 4.2: Adding Tiles to Pentominos *(pages 36–37)*

Resource Options for Planning

	Suggested Pacing	Assignment Guide (ACE questions)	Materials for Students	Resources for Teachers
Investigation 4	2 days total	Exercises are in Student Edition pp. 38–44	■ calculators ■ square tiles (24 per group) ■ centimeter grid paper	■ Additional Practice, Investigation 4 , (TG, p. 153) ■ Centimeter grid paper BLM (TG, p. 145)
Problem 4.1	1 day	1–14	■ Labsheet 4.ACE (1 per student) ■ inch grid paper	■ Transparency 4.1 (TG, p. 129) * ■ Labsheet 4.ACE (TG, p. 116) ■ Inch grid paper BLM (TG, p. 148)
Problem 4.2	1 day	15		■ Transparency 4.2 (TG, p. 130) *
Mathematical Reflections		MR 1–3	■ journal	

* optional materials

© Prentice-Hall, Inc.

Investigation 5: Measuring Parallelograms

Mathematical and Problem-Solving Goals

- To discover relationships between parallelograms and rectangles

- To use relationships between rectangles and parallelograms to develop techniques or formulas for finding areas and perimeters of parallelograms

- To apply techniques for finding areas and perimeters of rectangles and parallelograms to a variety of problem situations

Problems in this Investigation

Problem 5.1: Finding Measures of Parallelograms *(pages 46–48)*

Problem 5.2: Designing Parallelograms Under Constraints *(pages 48–49)*

Problem 5.3: Rearranging Parallelograms *(page 50)*

Resource Options for Planning

	Suggested Pacing	Assignment Guide (ACE questions)	Materials for Students	Resources for Teachers
Investigation 5	3 days total	Exercises are in Student Edition, pp. 51–54	■ calculators	■ Additional Practice, Investigation 5 (TG, p. 154) ■ transparency of centimeter grid paper * ■ Centimeter grid paper BLM (TG, p. 145)
Problem 5.1	1 day	12	■ Labsheet 5.1	■ Transparency 5.1 (TG, p. 131) * ■ Labsheet 5.1 BLM (TG p. 117)
Problem 5.2	1 day	8, 15	■ centimeter grid paper	■ Centimeter grid paper BLM (TG, p. 145)
Problem 5.3	1 day	1–7, 9–11, 13, 14, 16	■ centimeter grid paper ■ centimeter rulers ■ scissors	■ Centimeter grid paper BLM (TG, p. 145)
Mathematical Reflections		MR 1, 2	■ journal	

* optional materials

© Prentice-Hall, Inc.

Lesson Planner

Investigation 6: Measuring Triangles

Mathematical and Problem-Solving Goals

■ To find relationships between triangles and parallelograms

■ To use the relationships between rectangles and parallelograms and between parallelograms and triangles to develop techniques for finding area and perimeters of triangles

■ To apply techniques for finding areas and perimeters of rectangles, parallelograms, and triangles to a variety of problem situations

Problems in this Investigation

Problem 6.1: Finding Measures of Triangles *(pages 56–57)*

Problem 6.2: Designing Triangles Under Constraints *(pages 58–59)*

Problem 6.3: Making Parallelograms from Triangles *(page 59)*

Resource Options for Planning

	Suggested Pacing	Assignment Guide (ACE questions)	Materials for Students	Resources for Teachers
Investigation 6	4 days total	Exercises are in Student Edition, pp. 60–67	■ calculators	■ Additional Practice, Investigation 6 (TG, p. 155) ■ transparency of centimeter grid paper * ■ Centimeter grid paper BLM (TG, p. 145)
Problem 6.1	1 day	Unassigned choices from earlier problems	■ Labsheet 6.1	■ Transparency 6.1 (TG, p. 134) * ■ Labsheet 6.1 (TG, p. 118)
Problem 6.2	1 day	7	■ centimeter grid paper	■ Transparency 6.2 (TG, p. 135) * ■ Centimeter grid paper BLM (TG, p. 145)
Problem 6.3	2 days	1–6, 8–11, 21, 22	■ centimeter grid paper ■ scissors ■ centimeter rulers ■ tape ■ inch grid paper * ■ construction paper *	■ Transparency 6.3 (TG, p. 136) * ■ Centimeter grid paper BLM (TG, p. 145) ■ inch grid paper (TG, p. 148) *
Mathematical Reflections		MR 1–3	■ journal	

* optional materials

© Prentice-Hall, Inc.

Investigation 7: Going Around in Circles

Mathematical and Problem-Solving Goals

- To develop techniques for estimating the area of a circle
- To discover that it takes slightly more than three diameters to equal the circumference of a circle
- To discover that it takes slightly more than three radius squares to equal the area of a circle
- To use ideas about the area and perimeter to solve practical problems

Problems in this Investigation

Problem 7.1: Pricing Pizza *(page 70)*

Problem 7.2: Surrounding a Circle *(page 71)*

Problem 7.3: Covering a Circle *(pages 72–73)*

Problem 7.4: "Squaring" a Circle *(pages 73–74)*

Problem 7.5: Replacing Trees *(page 75)*

Resource Options for Planning

	Suggested Pacing	Assignment Guide (ACE questions)	Materials for Students	Resources for Teachers
Investigation 7	6 days total	Exercises are in Student Edition, pp. 76–80	■ calculators ■ compasses (1 per student) ■ centimeter grid paper	■ Additional Practice, Investigation 7 (TG, p. 156) ■ Centimeter grid paper BLM (TG, p. 145)
Problem 7.1	1 day	14	■ string ■ scissors	■ Transparency 7.1 (TG, p. 137) * ■ 9-cm, 12-cm and 15-cm circles cut from transparent grid paper *
Problem 7.2	1 day	1–5 (circumference only), 6–8	■ several circular objects ■ tape measure	■ Transparency 7.2 (TG, p. 138) *
Problem 7.3	1 day	Unassigned choices from earlier problems		■ Transparency 7.3 (TG, p. 139) *
Problem 7.4	1 day	1–13	■ Labsheet 7.4 (1 per student) ■ scissors	■ Transparency 7.4 (TG, p. 140) * ■ Labsheet 7.4 BLM (TG, p. 119)
Problem 7.5	2 days	16, 17		■ Transparency 7.5 (TG, p. 141) *
Mathematical Reflections		MR 1–2	■ journal	

* optional materials

© Prentice-Hall, Inc.

Unit Organizer

How Likely Is It?

Pacing Options

Investigations and Assessments	Class Time (days)
1 A First Look at Chance (SE, pp. 5–13)	2
2 More Experiements with Chance (SE, pp. 14–21)	2
3 Using Spinners to Predict Chances (SE, pp. 22–28)	2
Quiz (TG, pp. 69–70)	1
Check-Up 1 (TG, pp. 67–68)	1
4 Theoretical Probabilities (SE, pp. 29–41)	3
5 Analyzing Games of Chance (SE, pp. 42–48)	2
6 More About Games of Chance (SE, pp. 49–56)	2
7 Probability and Genetics (SE, pp. 57–64)	3
Looking Back and Looking Ahead: Unit Reflections (SE, pp. 65–67)	1
Check-Up 2 (TG, pp. 71–72)	1/2
Self-Assessment (TG, p. 79)	take home
Unit Test (TG, pp. 74–77)	1

Teacher's Guide and Ancillary Resources

Assessment Resources (pp. 65–88)

Blackline Masters (pp. 89–108)

Additional Practice (pp. 109–116)

 Assessment and Additional Practice

Essential Vocabulary

certain event	impossible event
chances	
equally likely events	outcome
event	probability
experimental probability	theoretical probability

Prerequisite Units

Prime Time (Number and Operations)

Data About Us (Data Analysis and Probability)

Bits and Pieces I (Number and Operations)

NCTM Principles and Standards 2000

Content Standard: Data Analysis and Probability

Process Standards: Problem Solving, Reasoning and Proof, Communication, Connections, and Representation

Materials

Pennies (3 per pair or group)

Number cubes (1 per pair)

Large and small marshmallows (10 of each size per pair or group)

Game markers, such as buttons (12 per pair)

Bobby pins or paper clips (for making spinner; 1 per pair or group)

Game chips (3 per student; for the Quiz and Unit Test)

Sheets of card stock

Paper cups (1 per pair or group; optional)

Computer and the Coin Game program (see "Technology" on TG page 1g; optional)

Blocks or other objects (in 3 colors; optional)

Opaque bucket or bag (2 per group; optional)

Opaque container with blocks (9 red, 6 yellow, 3 blue)

Mathematics in the Unit

- Become acquainted with probability informally through experiments.
- Understand that probabilities are useful for predicting what will happen over the long run.
- Understand that probabilities are useful for making decisions.
- Understand the two ways to obtain probabilities: by gathering data from experiments (experimental probability) and by analyzing the possible equally likely outcomes (theoretical probability).
- Understand the concepts of equally likely and unequally likely.
- Understand the relationship between experimental and theoretical probabilities: experimental probabilities are better estimates of theoretical probabilities when they are based on a larger number of trials.
- Determine and critically interpret statements of probability.
- Develop strategies for finding both experimental and theoretical probabilities.
- Organize data into lists or charts of equally likely oucomes as a strategy for finding theoretical probabilities. (Other strategies, such as tree diagrams and the area model, will be introduced in the grade 7 probability unit, *What Do You Expect?*)
- Use graphs and tallies to summarize and display data.
- Use data displayed in graphs and tallies to find experimental probabilities.

© Prentice-Hall, Inc.

Connections to Other Units

The ideas in *How Likely Is It?* build on and connect to several big ideas in other Connected Mathematics units.

Big Idea	Prior Work	Future Work
developing understanding of probability	performing operations with whole numbers; finding factors and multiples *(Prime Time)*; developing understanding of ratio in fraction, percent, or decimal form *(Bits and Pieces I)*	applying rational numbers *(Bits and Pieces II, Comparing and Scaling)*; finding probabilities and expected values for more complex games and situations *(What Do You Expect?)*; using probabilities to make inferences and predictions *(Samples and Populations)*; developing counting strategies to help determine probabilities *(Clever Counting)*
determining experimental probabilities	collecting and organizing data *(Data About Us)*; working with ratio and proportion *(Bits and Pieces I)*	collecting and organizing data from complex games and situations to determine experimental probabilities *(What Do You Expect?)*; using experimental probabilities to make inferences and predictions *(Samples and Populations, Clever Counting)*
determining theoretical probabilities	analyzing games or situations *(Prime Time)*; identifying and organizing all possible outcomes and looking for patterns *(Data About Us, Covering and Surrounding)*; working with ratio and proportion *(Bits and Pieces I)*	devising strategies for finding and applying theoretical probabilities *(What Do You Expect?)*; making inferences and predictions using theoretical probabilities *(Samples and Populations)*; developing counting strategies to determine theoretical probabilities *(Clever Counting)*
developing understanding of randomness	identifying and organizing all possible outcomes of a game or situation and looking for patterns *(Data About Us, Covering and Surrounding)*; working with ratio and proportion *(Bits and Pieces I)*	analyzing and comparing games and situations in which outcomes are random or biased *(What Do You Expect?)*; selecting and analyzing random samples to make inferences and predictions about a larger population *(Samples and Populations)*

© Prentice-Hall, Inc.

Investigation 1: A First Look at Chance

Mathematical and Problem-Solving Goals

- To build intuition that probability, or chance, has to do with events that are uncertain but that have a pattern of regularity over the long run

- To determine relative frequencies from experimental data and use them to predict behavior over the long run

- To observe that small numbers of trials may produce wide variation in results

- To display collected data in graphs or tallies and use them to find experimental probabilities

- To recognize equally likely events

Problems in this Investigation

Problem 1.1: Flipping for Breakfast *(pages 5–6)*

Problem 1.2: Analyzing Events *(pages 7–8)*

Resource Options for Planning

	Suggested Pacing	Assignment Guide (ACE questions)	Materials for Students	Resources for Teachers
Investigation 1	2 days total	Exercises are in Student Edition, pp. 9–12	■ calculators	■ Additional Practice, Investigation 1 (TG, p. 110)
Problem 1.1	1 day	1–5, 15	■ Labsheets 1.1A and 1.1B (1 per group) ■ pennies (1 per group) ■ paper cup (1 per group) *	■ Transparency 1.1 (TG, p. 95) * ■ Labsheets 1.1A and 1.1B BLM (TG, pp. 90, 91) ■ A computer and the Coin Game *
Problem 1.2	1 day	6–14		■ Transparency 1.2 (TG, p. 96) *
Mathematical Reflections		MR 1–4	■ journal	

* optional materials

© Prentice-Hall, Inc.

Investigation 2: More Experiments with Chance

Mathematical and Problem-Solving Goals

■ To gain experience finding experimental probabilities of unequally likely events

■ To understand that chance (probability) is an *estimate* of behavior over the long run

■ To understand that to make good decisions based on experimental probabilities, the probabilities must be based on a large number of trials

■ To understand that a game of chance is fair only if each player has the same chance of winning, not just a possible chance of winning

Problems in this Investigation

Problem 2.1: Testing Paper Bridges *(pages 14–15)*

Problem 2.2: Drawing Graph Models *(page 16)*

Resource Options for Planning

	Suggested Pacing	Assignment Guide (ACE questions)	Materials for Students	Resources for Teachers
Investigation 2	2 days total	Exercises are in Student Edition, pp. 17–20	■ calculators	■ Additional Practice, Investigation 2 (TG, p. 111)
Problem 2.1	1 day	29–31	■ large and small marshmallows (10 of each size per group) ■ paper cups (1 per group) *	■ Transparency 2.1 (TG, p. 97) *
Problem 2.2 **Mathematical Reflections**	1 day	25, 28 MR 1–4	■ pennies (3 per group) ■ journal	■ Transparency 2.2 (TG, p. 98) *

* optional materials

© Prentice-Hall, Inc.

Lesson Planner

Investigation 3: Using Spinners to Predict Chances

Mathematical and Problem-Solving Goals

■ To develop strategies for finding experimental probabilities with a new simulation tool: spinners

■ To understand that to make good decisions based on experimental probabilities, the probabilities must be based on a large number of trials

Problems in this Investigation

Problem 3.1: Bargaining for a Better Bedtime *(pages 22–23)*

Resource Options for Planning

	Suggested Pacing	Assignment Guide (ACE questions)	Materials for Students	Resources for Teachers
Investigation 3	2 days total	Exercises are in Student Edition, pp. 24–27	■ calculators	■ Additional Practice, Investigation 3 (TG, p. 112)
Problem 3.1	2 days	1–12	■ Labsheet 3.1 (1 per group) ■ bobby pins or paper clips (1 per group) ■ Labsheet 3.ACE	■ Transparency 3.1 (TG, p. 99) * ■ Labsheet 3.ACE BLM (TG, p. 93)
Mathematical Reflections		MR 1–4	■ journal	

* optional materials

© Prentice-Hall, Inc.

Lesson Planner

Investigation 4: Theoretical Probabilities

Mathematical and Problem-Solving Goals

■ To understand the two ways to obtain probabilities: by gathering data from experiments (experimental probability) and by analyzing possible and favorable outcomes (theoretical probability)

■ To understand the relationship between experimental and theoretical probabilities: when an experimental probability is based on a large number of trials, it is a good estimate of the theoretical probability

■ To develop strategies for finding theoretical probabilities, such as making an organized list of all possible outcomes

■ To develop an understanding of the word *random*

Problems in this Investigation

Problem 4.1: Predicting to Win *(pages 29–31)*

Problem 4.2: Drawing More Blocks *(page 32)*

Problem 4.3: Winning the Bonus Prize *(pages 33–34)*

Resource Options for Planning

	Suggested Pacing	Assignment Guide (ACE questions)	Materials for Students	Resources for Teachers
Investigation 4	3 days total	Exercises are in Student Edition, pp. 35–40	■ Grid paper ■ Graphing calculators	■ Additional Practice, Investigation 4 (TG, p. 113)
Problem 4.1	1 day	1, 2, 4		■ Transparency 4.1 (TG, p. 100) * ■ Opaque bucket or bag filled with 9 red blocks, 6 yellow blocks, and 3 blue blocks
Problem 4.2	1 day	3, 5, 6	■ Opaque containers filled with 4 red blocks, 3 yellow blocks, and 1 blue block (1 per group) *	■ Transparency 4.2 (TG, p. 101) * ■ Opaque bucket or bag filled with 4 red blocks, 3 yellow blocks, and 1 blue block
Problem 4.3	1 day	7–9	■ Opaque containers filled with 2 red blocks, 2 yellow blocks, and 2 blue blocks (1 per group) *	■ Transparency 4.3 (TG, p. 102) * ■ Two opaque containers, each containing 1 red block, 1 yellow block, and 1 blue block
Mathematical Reflections		MR 1–5	■ journal	

* optional materials

© Prentice-Hall, Inc.

Lesson Planner

Investigation 5: Analyzing Games of Chance

Mathematical and Problem-Solving Goals

- To understand the two ways to obtain probabilities: by gathering data from experiments (experimental probability) and by analyzing possible and favorable outcomes (theoretical probability)

- To develop strategies for finding theoretical probabilities, such as making an organized list of all possible outcomes

- To gain a better understanding of what it means for events to be equally likely in situations in which individual outcomes are combined to obtain the events of interest

Problems in this Investigation

Problem 5.1: Playing Roller Derby *(pages 42–43)*

Resource Options for Planning				
	Suggested Pacing	**Assignment Guide** (ACE questions)	**Materials for Students**	**Resources for Teachers**
Investigation 5	2 days total	Exercises are in Student Edition, pp. 44–47		■ Additional Practice, Investigation 5 (TG, p. 114)
Problem 5.1	2 days	1–18	■ calculators ■ Labsheet 5.1 (1 per pair) ■ number cubes (2 per pair) ■ game markers (12 per pair) ■ journal	■ Transparency 5.1 (TG, p. 103) * ■ Labsheet 5.1 BLM (TG p. 94) ■ game markers ■ number cubes (2 different colors) *
Mathematical Reflections		MR 1–4		

* optional materials

© Prentice-Hall, Inc.

Investigation 6: More About Games of Chance

Mathematical and Problem-Solving Goals

- To gain experience in choosing appropriate simulation strategies
- To understand, find, and compare experimental and theoretical probabilities
- To gain experience in critically analyzing and interpreting probabilistic statements

Problems in this Investigation

Problem 6.1: Scratching Spots *(pages 49–50)*

Resource Options for Planning

	Suggested Pacing	Assignment Guide (ACE questions)	Materials for Students	Resources for Teachers
Investigation 6	2 days total	Exercises are in Student Edition, pp. 51–55		■ Additional Practice, Investigation 6 (TG, p. 115)
Problem 6.1	2 days	1–4 Options: see TG, p. 49	■ calculators ■ materials for simulating the contest, such as blocks, spinners, and sheets of card stock for making cards	■ Transparency 6.1 (TG, p. 104) * ■ scratch-off game card *
Mathematical Reflections		MR 1–3	■ journal	

* optional materials

© Prentice-Hall, Inc.

Lesson Planner

Investigation 7: Probability and Genetics

Mathematical and Problem-Solving Goals

■ To increase understanding of experimental and theoretical probability

■ To appreciate the power of probability for making predictions and decisions

Problems in this Investigation

Problem 7.1: Curling Your Tongue *(pages 57–58)*

Problem 7.2: Tracing Traits *(pages 58–60)*

Resource Options for Planning

	Suggested Pacing	Assignment Guide (ACE questions)	Materials for Students	Resources for Teachers
Investigation 7	3 days total	Exercises are in Student Edition, pp. 61–63	■ calculators	■ Additional Practice, Investigation 7 (TG, p. 116)
Problem 7.1	1 day	7, 8a, 8b		■ Transparency 7.1 (TG, p. 105) *
Problem 7.2	2 days	1–6, 9		■ Transparency 7.2 (TG, p. 106) *
Mathematical Reflections		MR 1–3	■ journal	

* optional materials

© Prentice-Hall, Inc.

Bits and Pieces II

Pacing Options

Investigations and Assessments	Class Time (days)
1 Using Percents (SE, pp. 5–17)	5
2 More About Percents (SE, pp. 18–30)	4
Check-Up 1 (TG, p. 79)	1/2
3 Estimating With Fractions and Decimals (SE, pp. 31–42)	2
4 Adding and Subtracting Fractions (SE, pp. 43–53)	5
Check-Up 2 (TG, pp. 80–81)	1/2
5 Finding Areas and Other Products (SE, pp. 54–63)	4
6 Computing with Decimals (SE, pp. 64–76)	5
Check-Up 3 (TG, pp. 82–83)	1/2
7 Dividing Fractions (SE, pp. 77–87)	5
Looking Back and Looking Ahead: Unit Reflections (SE, pp. 88–90)	1
Self-Assessment (TG, p. 94)	take home
Unit Test (TG, pp. 87–92)	1

Teacher's Guide and Ancillary Resources

Assessment Resources (pp. 77–103)

Blackline Masters (pp. 105–141)

Additional Practice (pp. 143–151, 163)

 Assessment and Additional Practice

Essential Vocabulary

decimal

denominator

equivalent fractions

fraction

numerator

percent

Prerequisite Units

Prime Time (Number and Operations)

Bits and Pieces I (Number and Operations)

NCTM Principles and Standards 2000

Content Standard: Number and Operations

Process Standards: Problem Solving, Reasoning and Proof, Communication, Connections, and Representation

Materials

Calculators

Getting Close cards (provided as BLM)

Getting Close number squares (provided as BLM)

Hundredths grids (provided as BLM)

Hundredths strips (provided as BLM)

Sheet of squares (provided as BLM)

Marker, tiles, or paper squares (about 12 per student)

Angle rulers

Colored square tiles (optional)

Mathematics in the Unit

- Continue to build understanding of fractions, decimals, and percents and the relationships among these concepts and their representations.
- Use strategies to quickly estimate sums and products.
- Use 0, $\frac{1}{2}$, 1, $1\frac{1}{2}$, and 2 as benchmarks to make sense of how large a sum is.
- Develop strategies for adding, subtracting, multiplying, and dividing fractions and decimals.
- Understand when addition, subtraction, multiplication, or division is the appropriate operation.
- Become facile at changing a fraction to a decimal and at estimating what fraction a given decimal is near.
- Explore the relationship between two numbers and their product to generalize the conditions under which the product is greater than both factors, between the factors, or less than both factors.
- Use percent as an expression of frequency when a data set does not contain exactly 100 pieces of data.
- Represent $1.00 as 100 pennies so that a special application of the hundredths grid can be used to visualize percents of a dollar.
- Use percents to compute taxes, tips, and discounts.
- Develop models to represent a situation. Example: show that $\frac{1}{2}$ of $\frac{1}{2}$ is $\frac{1}{4}$ by drawing an area model.
- Use context to help reason about the problem.

© Prentice-Hall, Inc.

Connections to Other Units

The ideas in *Bits and Pieces II* build on and connect to several big ideas in other Connected Mathematics units.

Big Idea	Prior Work	Future Work
performing computations involving percents	defining, comparing, and applying percents *(Bits and Pieces I)*; interpreting percents as probabilities *(How Likely Is It?)*	using percents to make comparisons *(Comparing and Scaling)*; interpreting percents as probabilities *(What Do You Expect?, Samples and Populations)*; applying percents to analyze data *(Data Around Us)*
performing mathematical operations with fractions	interpreting fractions as part/whole relationships; combining and comparing fractions; finding equivalent fractions *(Bits and Pieces I)*; interpreting fractions as probabilities *(How Likely Is It?)*	interpreting fractions as scale factors, ratios, and proportions *(Stretching and Shrinking, Comparing and Scaling)*; interpreting fractions as constants and variable coefficients in linear and nonlinear equations and relationships *(Variables and Patterns; Moving Straight Ahead; Thinking with Mathematical Models; Growing, Growing, Growing; Frogs, Fleas, and Painted Cubes; Say It With Symbols)*; using fractions to help understand irrational numbers *(Looking for Pythagoras)*; interpreting and applying fractions *(What Do You Expect?, Samples and Populations)*
performing mathematical operations with decimals	interpreting decimals as fractions; understanding place value of decimals; combining and comparing decimals *(Bits and Pieces I)*; interpreting decimals as probabilities *(How Likely Is It?)*	interpreting decimals as ratios and proportions *(Comparing and Scaling)*; exploring the relationship between repeating decimals and irrational numbers *(Looking for Pythagoras)*; interpreting decimals as probabilities *(What Do You Expect?, Samples and Populations)*; using decimals in scientific notation *(Data Around Us)*; interpreting decimals as coefficients in linear and nonlinear equations *(Variables and Patterns; Moving Straight Ahead; Thinking with Mathematical Models; Growing, Growing, Growing; Frogs, Fleas, and Painted Cubes; Say It With Symbols)*
developing and applying algorithms for performing calculations with fractions, decimals, and percents	connecting fractions, decimals, and percents; estimating to check reasonableness of answers *(Bits and Pieces I)*; developing algorithms for finding the area and perimeter of 2-D shapes *(Covering and Surrounding)*	applying decimals, fractions, and percents in studying probability *(What Do You Expect?, Samples and Populations)*; applying ratios, proportions, and scale factors *(Stretching and Shrinking, Comparing and Scaling)*

© Prentice-Hall, Inc.

Investigation 1: Using Percents

Mathematical and Problem-Solving Goals

■ To use the "out of 100" interpretation to develop an understanding of the concept of percent

■ To think about representing $1.00 as 100 pennies and to relate this to the hundredths-grid model as a way of visualize the percent of a dollar

■ To use percent in estimating or computing taxes, tips, and discounts

Problems in this Investigation

Problem 1.1: Taxing Tapes *(pages 5–7)*

Problem 1.2: Computing Tips *(pages 7–8)*

Problem 1.3: Finding Bargains *(pages 9–10)*

Problem 1.4: Spending Money *(pages 10–11)*

Resource Options for Planning

	Suggested Pacing	Assignment Guide (ACE questions)	Materials for Students	Resources for Teachers
Investigation 1	5 days total	Exercises are in Student Edition, pp. 12–16	■ calculators	■ Additional Practice, Investigation 1 (TG, p. 144)
Problem 1.1	1 day	1, 5, 10, 19–22	■ hundredths grids	■ Transparency 1.1 (TG, p. 110) * ■ Hundredths grids BLM (TG, p. 135)
Problem 1.2	1 day	2, 3, 18, 30–33	■ Labsheets 1.2A and 1.2B (1 each per group) ■ transparencies of Labsheet1.2B * ■ transparency markers	■ Transparency 1.2 (TG, p. 111) ■ Labsheets 1.2A and 1.2B BLM (TG, pp. 106–107)
Problem 1.3	1 day	4, 6–9, 8–17, 29		■ Transparency 1.3 (TG, p. 112) *
Problem 1.4 **Mathematical Reflections**	2 days	Unassigned choices from earlier problems MR 1–4	■ journal	■ Transparency 1.4 (TG, p. 113) *

* optional materials

© Prentice-Hall, Inc.

Investigation 2: More About Percents

Mathematical and Problem-Solving Goals

- To use the "out of 100" interpretation to develop an understanding of the concept of percent
- To investigate the relationships among fractions, decimals, and percents
- To understand how to use precent as an expression of frequency in terms of "out of 100" when a set of data contains more than or less than 100 pieces of data

Problems in this Investigation

Problem 2.1: Finding Percents *(pages 18–19)*

Problem 2.2: Finding a General Strategy *(page 19)*

Problem 2.3: Clipping Coupons *(pages 20–21)*

Problem 2.4: Making Circle Graphs *(pages 21–23)*

Resource Options for Planning

	Suggested Pacing	Assignment Guide (ACE questions)	Materials for Students	Resources for Teachers
Investigation 2	4 days total	Exercises are in Student Edition, pp. 24–29	■ calculators	■ Additional Practice, Investigation 2 (TG, p. 145)
Problem 2.1	1 day	1–4, 11, 17–21	■ hundredths grids	■ Transparency 2.1 (TG, p. 114) * ■ Hundredths grids BLM (TG, p. 135)
Problem 2.2	1 day	12, 14–15, 26–30	■ hundredths grids ■ hundredths strips	■ Transparency 2.2 (TG, p. 115) * ■ Hundredths grids BLM (TG, p. 135) ■ Hundredths strips BLM (TG, p. 136)
Problem 2.3	1 day	13, 23, 24		■ Transparency 2.3 (TG, p. 116) *
Problem 2.4 **Mathematical Reflections**	1 day	5–10, 16, 25 MR 1–3	■ angle rulers ■ large sheets of paper * ■ journal	■ Transparency 2.4 (TG, p. 117) *

* optional materials

© Prentice-Hall, Inc.

Lesson Planner

Investigation 3: Estimating with Fractions and Decimals

Mathematical and Problem-Solving Goals

- To develop strategies for estimating sums of fractions and decimals
- To make sense of whether a situation requires an overestimate or an underestimate
- To use 0, $\frac{1}{2}$, 1, $1\frac{1}{2}$, and 2 as benchmarks to make sense of the size of a sum
- To use estimation strategies to quickly approximate a particular sum

Problems in this Investigation

Problem 3.1: Getting Close *(pages 31–33)*

Problem 3.2: Getting Even Closer *(pages 33–34)*

Resource Options for Planning

	Suggested Pacing	Assignment Guide (ACE questions)	Materials for Students	Resources for Teachers
Investigation 3	2 days total	Exercises are in Student Edition, pp. 35–41	■ calculators ■ Getting Close cards (1 set per group) ■ Getting Close number squares (1 set per student) ■ hundredths grids ■ hundredths strips	■ Additional Practice, Investigation 3 (TG, p. 146) ■ Getting Close cards BLM (TG, pp. 137–138) ■ Getting Close number squares BLM (TG, p. 139) ■ Hundredths grids BLM (TG, p. 135) ■ Hundredths strips BLM (TG, p. 136)
Problem 3.1	1 day	1–10, 35–36, 38–43		■ Transparency 3.1 (TG, p. 118) *
Problem 3.2	1 day	11–34, 37		■ Transparency 3.2 (TG, p. 119) *
Mathematical Reflections		MR 1–3	■ journal	

* optional materials

© Prentice-Hall, Inc.

Lesson Planner

Investigation 4: Adding and Subtracting Fractions

Mathematical and Problem-Solving Goals

- To develop strategies for adding and subtracting fractions
- To understand when addition or subtraction is the appropriate operation
- To develop ways of modeling sums and differences
- To continue to develop ways to estimate the results of adding or subtracting fractions
- To reinforce understanding of equivalence of fractions
- To employ pictorial models (for example, showing that $\frac{1}{2}$ of $\frac{1}{2}$ is $\frac{1}{4}$ by drawing an area model)
- To search for and to generalize patterns
- To use estimation to help make decisions

Problems in this Investigation

Problem 4.1: Dividing Land *(pages 43–44)*

Problem 4.2: Redrawing the Map *(pages 44–45)*

Problem 4.3: Pirating Pizza *(pages 46–47)*

Problem 4.4: Designing Algorithms *(page 48)*

Resource Options for Planning

	Suggested Pacing	Assignment Guide (ACE questions)	Materials for Students	Resources for Teachers
Investigation 4	5 days total	Exercises are in Student Edition, pp. 49–52	■ calculators	■ Additional Practice, Investigation 4 (TG, p. 147)
Problem 4.1	1 day	10–26	■ Labsheet 4.1 (1 per student) ■ rulers	■ Transparency 4.1 (TG, p. 120) * ■ Labsheet 4.1 BLM (TG, p. 108)
Problem 4.2	1 day	1, 3	■ Labsheet 4.1 (1 per student) ■ grid paper ■ colored square tiles	■ Transparency 4.2 (TG, p. 121) * ■ Grid paper BLM (TG, p. 141) ■ Labsheet 4.1 BLM (TG, p. 108)
Problem 4.3	1 day	2, 4		■ Transparency 4.3 (TG, p. 122) *
Problem 4.4	2 days	5–9, 27	■ Large sheets of paper or blank transparencies *	■ Transparency 4.4 (TG, p. 123) *
Mathematical Reflections		MR 1–3	■ journal	

* optional materials

© Prentice-Hall, Inc.

Investigation 5: Finding Areas and Other Products

Mathematical and Problem-Solving Goals

- To develop an understanding of multiplication of fractions
- To use an area model to represent the product of two fractions
- To find a fraction of a whole number
- To explore the relationship between two numbers and their product
- To use estimation as a way to make sense of products
- To draw pictures to represent problem stiuations
- To search for and to generalize patterns
- To use a problem's context to help reason about the answer

Problems in this Investigation

Problem 5.1: Selling Brownies *(pages 54–55)*

Problem 5.2: Discounting Brownie*s (pages 56–57)*

Problem 5.3: Buying the Biggest Lot *(page 58)*

Problem 5.4: Designing a Multiplication Algorithm *(page 59)*

Resource Options for Planning

	Suggested Pacing	**Assignment Guide** (ACE questions)	**Materials for Students**	**Resources for Teachers**
Investigation 5	4 days total	Exercises are in Student Edition, pp. 60–62	■ calulators ■ large sheets of paper or sheets of blank transparency film *	■ Additional Practice, Investigation 5 (TG, p. 148)
Problem 5.1	1 day	11–17	■ sheets of squares	■ Transparency 5.1 (TG, p. 124) * ■ Sheet of squares BLM (TG, p. 140)
Problem 5.2	1 day	1–5	■ sheets of squares	■ Transparency 5.2 (TG, p. 125) * ■ Sheet of squares BLM (TG, p. 140)
Problem 5.3	1 day	6, 19		■ Transparency 5.3 (TG, p. 126) *
Problem 5.4	1 day	7–10, 18, 20		■ Transparency 5.4 (TG, p. 127) *
Mathematical Reflections		MR 1–3	■ journal	

* optional materials

© Prentice-Hall, Inc.

Investigation 6: Computing with Decimals

Mathematical and Problem-Solving Goals

- To explore situations that involve operations with decimals
- To use strategies for quickly estimating sums and products
- To develop strategies for adding and subtracting decimals
- To understand when addition or subtraction is the appropriate operation
- To look for and to generalize patterns
- To develop an understanding of decimal multiplication
- To use estimation to help make decisions
- To use a problem's context to help reason about answers

Problems in this Investigation

Problem 6.1: Buying School Supplies *(pages 64–66)*

Problem 6.2: Moving Decimal Points *(pages 66–68)*

Problem 6.3: Multiplying Decimals *(pages 68–69)*

Problem 6.4: Shifting Decimal Points *(page 70)*

Problem 6.5: Fencing a Yard *(page 71)*

Resource Options for Planning

	Suggested Pacing	Assignment Guide (ACE questions)	Materials for Students	Resources for Teachers
Investigation 6	5 days total	*Exercises are in Student Edition, pp. 72–75	■ calculators	■ Additional Practice, Investigation 6 (TG, p. 149)
Problem 6.1	1 day	1–3, 5	■ Labsheet 6.1 (1 per pair) ■ markers, tiles, or paper squares (about 15 per student)	■ Transparency 6.1 (TG, p. 128) * ■ Labsheet 6.1 BLM (TG, p. 109)
Problem 6.2	1 day	4, 6		■ Transparency 6.2 (TG, p. 129) *
Problem 6.3	1 day	5, 7–10		■ Transparency 6.3 (TG, p. 130) *
Problem 6.4	1 day	11, 12		■ Transparency 6.4 (TG, p. 131) *
Problem 6.5	1 day	13	■ grid paper (1 sheet per student)	■ Transparency 6.5 (TG, p. 132) * ■ Grid paper BLM (TG, p. 141)
Mathematical Reflections		MR 1–6	■ journal	

* optional materials

© Prentice-Hall, Inc.

Investigation 7: Dividing Fractions

Mathematical and Problem-Solving Goals

- To develop the meaning of division with fractions.
- To develop strategies and algorithms for dividing fractions.
- To recognize situations for which division is an appropriate operation.
- To explore the relationship between division and multiplication of fractions.

Problems in this Investigation

Problem 7.1: Fractions in Fund Raising *(pages 77–79)*

Problem 7.2: Share and Share Alike *(page 80)*

Problem 7.3: Summer Work *(pages 81–82)*

Resource Options for Planning

	Suggested Pacing	Assignment Guide (ACE questions)	Materials for Students	Resources for Teachers
Investigation 7	5 days total	Exercises are in Student Edition, pp. 83–86		■ Additional Practice, Investigation 7 (TG, p. 163)
Problem 7.1	2 days	1–8, 19, 27–29, 44, 45		
Problem 7.2	1 day	9–13, 18, 20–23, 30–35, 43		
Problem 7.3 **Mathematical Reflections**	2 days	14–17, 24–26, 36–42, 46–48 MR 1–4	■ journal	

* optional materials

© Prentice-Hall, Inc.

Unit Organizer

Ruins of Montarek

Pacing Options

Investigations and Assessments	Class Time (days)
1 Building Plans (SE, pp. 7–25)	6
2 Making Buildings (SE, pp. 26–39)	3
3 Describing Unique Buildings (SE, pp. 40–51)	3
Check-Up 1 (TG, pp. 84–86)	1/2
4 Isometric Dot Paper Representations (SE, pp. 52–61)	4
5 Ziggurats (SE, pp. 62–71)	3
6 Seeing the Isometric View (SE, pp. 72–81)	4
Looking Back and Looking Ahead: Unit Reflections (SE, pp. 83–84)	1
Check-Up 2 (TG, pp. 87–89)	1/2
Quiz (TG, pp. 90–91)	1
Self-Assessment (TG, p. 100)	take home
Unit Test (TG, pp. 97–98)	1
Unit Project (SE, p. 82)	1

Teacher's Guide and Ancillary Resources

Assessment Resources (pp. 83–111)

Blackline Masters (pp. 113–151)

Additional Practice (pp. 153–159)

 Assessment and Additional Practice

Essential Vocabulary

base plan

maximal building

minimal building

set of building plans

Prerequisite Units

None

NCTM Principles and Standards 2000

Content Standard: Geometry

Process Standards: Problem Solving, Reasoning and Proof, Communication, Connections, and Representation

Materials

Cubes (20 per student)

Sugar cubes (optional)

Isometric dot paper (provided as BLM)

Rectangular dot paper (provided as BLM)

Envelopes (1 per student)

Angle rulers

Transparencies of isometric dot paper and grid paper

Interlocking cubes (optional)

Mathematics in the Unit

- Read and create two-dimensional representations of three-dimensional cube buildings.
- Communicate spatial information.
- Observe that the back view of a cube building is the mirror image of the front view and that the left view is the mirror image of the right view.
- Understand and recognize line symmetry.
- Explain how drawings of the base outline, front view, and right view describe a building.
- Construct cube buildings that fit two-dimensional building plans.
- Develop a way to describe all buildings that can be made from a set of plans.
- Understand that a set of plans can have more than one minimal building but only one maximal building.
- Explain how a cube can be represented on isometric dot paper, how the angles on the cube are represented with angles on the dot paper, and how the representations fit what the eye sees when viewing the corner of a cube building.
- Make isometric drawings of cube buildings.
- Visualize transformations of cube buildings and make isometric drawings of the transformed buildings.
- Reason about spatial relationships.
- Use models and representations of models to solve problems.

© Prentice-Hall, Inc.

Connections to Other Units

The ideas in *Ruins of Montarek* build on and connect to several big ideas in other
Connected Mathematics units.

Big Idea	Prior Work	Future Work
creating 2-D and 3-D representations and models of 3-D objects	exploring properties and measurements of 2-D figures; constructing models (with square tiles) of rectangles *(Shapes and Designs, Covering and Surrounding)*	finding surface area and volume of 3-D figures *(Filling and Wrapping)*; studying and developing mathematical models, including linear, exponential, and quadratic equations, counting trees, and neworks *(Thinking with Mathematical Models, Clever Counting)*
exploring relationships between 2-D and 3-D representations of 3-D objects (includes uniqueness of representations, maximal and minimal buildings)	exploring uniqueness of prime factorizations of integers *(Prime Time)*; investigating relationships between polygons *(Shapes and Designs)*	working with 2-D sketches and diagrams of 3-D figures; using 3-D models to study 3-D figures, including cones, cylinders, spheres, and prisms *(Filling and Wrapping)*
exploring symmetric properties of 2-D orthogonal views of 3-D cube buildings	exploring symmetry in 2-D shapes and polygons *(Shapes and Designs)*	exploring symmetry of graphs of functions *(Frogs, Fleas, and Painted Cubes)*; exploring symmetry of shapes subject to isometries *(Kaleidoscopes, Hubcaps, and Mirrors)*
interpreting and creating isometric views of 3-D objects	writing Logo programs that make specific shapes or shapes that meet specific conditions *(Shapes and Designs, Covering and Surrounding)*	visualizing and understanding properties of 3-D figures (e.g., cones, cylinders, spheres, prisms), including surface area as "wrapping" and volume as "filling" *(Filling and Wrapping)*; visualizing growth patterns in exponential and quadratic functions *(Growing, Growing, Growing; Frogs, Fleas, and Painted Cubes)*

© Prentice-Hall, Inc.

Investigation 1: Building Plans

Mathematical and Problem-Solving Goals

- To look at a cube building and see the orthogonal views without being distracted by depth perception

- To understand and use line symmetry (mirror symmetry)

- To discover that the base outline and the front and right views can be used to represent a cube building

- To draw sets of plans for cube buildings

- To match buildings to sets of building plans

Problems in this Investigation

Problem 1.1: Building from Base Plans *(pages 8–10)*

Problem 1.2: Reflecting Figures *(pages 10–12)*

Problem 1.3: Making Drawings of Cube Models *(page 13)*

Problem 1.4: Unraveling Mysteries *(page 14)*

Problem 1.5: Matching a Building to Its Plans *(pages 15–16)*

Problem 1.6: Which Building Is Which? *(pages 16–18)*

Resource Options for Planning

	Suggested Pacing	Assignment Guide (ACE questions)	Materials for Students	Resources for Teachers
Investigation 1	6 days total	Exercises are in Student Edition, pp. 19–24	■ calculators ■ cubes (20 per student) ■ building mat ■ grid paper ■ sugar cubes *	■ Additional Practice, Investigation 1 (TG, p. 154) ■ Grid paper BLM (TG, p. 149)
Problem 1.1	1 day	none		■ Transparency 1.1A (TG, p. 121) * ■ Transparency 1.1B (TG, p. 122) *
Problem 1.2	1 day	16, 17	■ Labsheets 1.2A and 1.2B (1 per student) ■ mirror ■ Labsheet 1.ACE	■ Transparency 1.2 (TG, p. 123) * ■ Labsheest 1.2A and 1.2B BLM (TG, pp. 114–115) ■ Labsheet 1.ACE BLM (TG, p. 116)
Problem 1.3	1 day	8		■ Transparency 1.3 (TG, p. 124) *
Problem 1.4	1 day	11, 12–15		■ Transparency 1.4 (TG, p. 125) *
Problem 1.5	1 day	1–4, 9, 10		■ Transparency 1.5A (TG, p. 126) * ■ Transparency 1.5B (TG, p. 127) *
Problem 1.6	1 day	5–7		■ Transparency 1.6A (TG, p. 128) * ■ Transparency 1.6B (TG, p. 129) *
Mathematical Reflections		MR 1–4	■ journal	

* optional materials

© Prentice-Hall, Inc.

Lesson Planner

Investigation 2: Making Buildings

Mathematical and Problem-Solving Goals

- To develop efficient strategies for reading a set of building plans and for constructing a building that matches a given set of plans

- To reason visually and analytically about cube buildings

- To make observations about similarities and differences in the buildings that fit a given set of plans or incomplete set of plans

Problems in this Investigation

Problem 2.1: Reconstructing Ruins *(pages 26–27)*

Problem 2.2: Constructing Buildings from Plans *(pages 28–30)*

Problem 2.3: Building from Incomplete Plans *(pages 30–32)*

Resource Options for Planning

	Suggested Pacing	Assignment Guide (ACE questions)	Materials for Students	Resources for Teachers
Investigation 2	3 days total	Exercises are in Student Edition, pp. 33–38	■ calculators ■ cubes (20 per student) ■ building mat ■ grid paper (about 6 sheets per student) ■ sugar cubes *	■ Grid paper BLM (TG, p. 149) ■ Additional Practice, Investigation 2 (TG, p. 155) ■ cubes ■ transparent grid
Problem 2.1	1 day	1, 2		■ Transparency 2.1 (TG, p. 130) *
Problem 2.2	1 day	7–10		■ Transparency 2.2A (TG, p. 131) * ■ Transparency 2.2B (TG, p. 132) *
Problem 2.3	1 day	3–6, 11, 12		■ Transparency 2.3 (TG, p. 133) *
Mathematical Reflections		MR 1–3	■ journal	

* optional materials

© Prentice-Hall, Inc.

Lesson Planner

Investigation 3: Describing Unique Buildings

Mathematical and Problem-Solving Goals

- To become proficient at reading a set of plans and constructing a building that matches a set of plans

- To reason visually and analytically about cube buildings

- To understand that several minimal buildings may fit a set of plans, but only one maximal building

- To develop a recording scheme to keep track of all buildings that fit a set of plans

Problems in this Investigation

Problem 3.1: Finding All the Possibilities *(pages 40–41)*

Problem 3.2: Finding Maximal and Minimal Buildings *(pages 41–42)*

Problem 3.3: Unraveling an Ancient Mystery *(pages 43–44)*

Resource Options for Planning

	Suggested Pacing	Assignment Guide (ACE questions)	Materials for Students	Resources for Teachers
Investigation 3	3 days total	Exercises are in Student Edition, pp. 45–50	■ calculators ■ cubes (20 per student) ■ building mat ■ grid paper (about 6 sheets per student) ■ sugar cubes *	■ Grid paper BLM (TG, p. 112) ■ cubes ■ transparent grid ■ Additional Practice, Investigation 3 (TG, p. 156)
Problem 3.1	1 day	5, 6	■ Labsheet 3.1 (1 per group)	■ Transparency 3.1 (TG, p. 134) * ■ Labsheet 3.1 BLM (TG, p. 117)
Problem 3.2	1 day	1–4	■ Labsheet 3.ACE (1 per student)	■ Transparency 3.2 (TG, p. 135) * ■ Labsheet 3.ACE BLM (TG, p. 93)
Problem 3.3	1 day	7, 8, 9–11		■ Transparency 3.3 (TG, p. 136) *
Mathematical Reflections		MR 1–3	■ journal	

* optional materials

© Prentice-Hall, Inc.

Investigation 4: Isometric Dot Paper Representations

Mathematical and Problem-Solving Goals

■ To understand how the dots are arranged on isometric dot paper and how this arrangement allows cube buildings to be drawn from corners

■ To visualize the relationship between the angles of an actual cube and an isometric drawing of a cube

■ To copy existing figures onto isometric dot paper

■ To construct buildings that fit isometric drawings and make isometric drawings of cube buildings

■ To use 2-D isometric models of cubes as design tools

■ To develop strategies for reading an isometric drawing and constructing a building that matches the drawing

■ To observe similarities and differences in buildings produced to fit isometric drawings

Problems in this Investigation

Problem 4.1: Drawing a Cube *(pages 53–54)*

Problem 4.2: Drawing a Cube Model *(pages 54–55)*

Problem 4.3: Drawing More Complex Buildings *(page 56)*

Problem 4.3: Creating Your Own Building *(page 57)*

Resource Options for Planning

	Suggested Pacing	Assignment Guide (ACE questions)	Materials for Students	Resources for Teachers
Investigation 4	4 days total	Exercises are in Student Edition, pp. 58–60	■ calculators ■ cubes (20 per student) ■ building mat ■ isometric dot paper ■ sugar cubes *	■ Isometric dot paper BLM (TG, p. 150) ■ Additional Practice, Investigation 4 (TG, p. 157)
Problem 4.1	1 day	none	■ angle rulers	■ Transparency 4.1 (TG, p. 137) *
Problem 4.2	1 day	1–4	■ Labsheet 4.2 (1 per student) ■ envelopes (1 per student) ■ scissors	■ Transparency 4.2 (TG, p. 138) * ■ Labsheet 4.2 BLM (TG, p. 118)
Problem 4.3	1 day	see TG, p. 56	■ paper or transparent graphing calculator grids *	■ Transparency 4.3 (TG, p. 139) *
Problem 4.4	1 day	5–7		■ Transparency 4.4 (TG, p. 140) *
Mathematical Reflections		MR 1–3	■ journal	

* optional materials

© Prentice-Hall, Inc.

Lesson Planner

Investigation 5: Ziggurats

Mathematical and Problem-Solving Goals

- To become more proficient at designing cube buildings and drawing isometric views
- To reason visually and analytically about cube buildings drawn on isometric dot paper
- To relate isometric drawings of buildings to sets of building plans
- To use patterns to reason about the number of cubes needed to build a given building

Problems in this Investigation

Problem 5.1: Building Ziggurats *(pages 62–63)*

Problem 5.2: Representing Ziggurats *(page 64)*

Resource Options for Planning

	Suggested Pacing	Assignment Guide (ACE questions)	Materials for Students	Resources for Teachers
Investigation 5	3 days total	Exercises are in Student Edition, pp. 65–70	■ calculators ■ cubes (20 per student) ■ building mats ■ isometric dot paper ■ sugar cubes *	■ Additional Practice, Investigation 5 (TG, p. 158) ■ cubes ■ transparent isometric dot paper ■ Isometric dot paper BLM (TG, p. 150)
Problem 5.1	1 day	1		■ Transparency 5.1 (TG, p. 141) *
Problem 5.2	2 days	2–4, 7, 8		■ Transparency 5.2 (TG, p. 142) *
Mathematical Reflections		MR 1–2	■ Journal	

* optional materials

© Prentice-Hall, Inc.

Investigation 6: Seeing the Isometric View

Mathematical and Problem-Solving Goals

- To develop an efficient strategy for reading information from isometric drawings in order to match buildings with their corner views

- To reason visually and analytically about cube buildings

- To visualize how a cube building will change when cubes are added or removed

- To solve visual puzzles by determining how two basic shapes can combine to form a given shape

- To create puzzles for others to solve

Problems in this Investigation

Problem 6.1: Viewing a Building *(pages 72–73)*

Problem 6.2: Removing Cubes *(page 74)*

Problem 6.3: Adding Cubes *(page 75)*

Problem 6.4: Putting the Pieces Together *(page 76)*

Resource Options for Planning

	Suggested Pacing	Assignment Guide (ACE questions)	Materials for Students	Resources for Teachers
Investigation 6	4 days total	Exercises are in Student Edition, pp. 77–80	■ calculators ■ cubes (20 per student) ■ building mat ■ isometric dot paper ■ sugar cubes * ■ 2-D design cubes (from Labsheet 4.2)	■ Additional Practice, Investigation 6 (TG, p. 159) ■ cubes ■ transparent isometric dot paper ■ Isometric dot paper BLM (TG, p. 150) ■ Labsheet 4.2 BLM (TG, p. 118)
Problem 6.1	1 day	1	■ Labsheet 6.1 (1 per student)	■ Transparency 6.1 (TG, p. 143) * ■ transparency of Labsheet 6.1 ■ Labsheet 6.1 BLM (TG, p. 119)
Problem 6.2	1 day	2, 5, 7		■ Transparency 6.2 (TG, p. 144) *
Problem 6.3	1 day	3		■ Transparency 6.3 (TG, p. 145) *
Problem 6.4	1 day	4, 6	■ Labsheet 6.4 (1 per student)	■ Transparency 6.4 (TG, p. 146) * ■ Labsheet 6.4 BLM (TG, p. 120)
Mathematical Reflections		MR 1–2	■ journal	■ interlocking cubes *

* optional materials

© Prentice-Hall, Inc.

Unit Organizer

Variables and Patterns

Pacing Options

Investigations and Assessments	Class Time (days)
1 Variables and Coordinate Graphs (SE, pp. 5–17) **2** Graphing Change (SE, pp. 18–35)	3 5
Check-Up (TG, pp. 70–72)	1/2
3 Analyzing Graphs and Tables (SE, pp. 36–48) **4** Patterns and Rules (SE, pp. 49–60)	4 3
Quiz (TG, pp. 73–75)	1
5 Using a Graphing Calculator (SE, pp. 61–68)	3
Looking Back and Looking Ahead: Unit Reflections (SE, pp. 69–70) Self-Assessment (TG, p. 84) Unit Test (TG, pp. 79–82)	1 1 1

Teacher's Guide and Ancillary Resources

Assessment Resources (pp. 69–97)

Blackline Masters (pp. 99–129)

Additional Practice (pp. 131–139)

Assessment and
Additional Practice

Essential Vocabulary

change	rule
coordinate graph	scale
coordinate pair	table
distance/time/rate	variable
of speed	*x*-axis
income/cost/profit	*x*-coordinate
pattern	*y*-axis
relationship	*y*-coordinate

Prerequisite Units

None

NCTM Principles and Standards 2000

Content Standard: Algebra

Process Standards: Problem Solving, Reasoning
and Proof, Communication, Connections,
and Representation

Materials

Graphing calculators

Clock or watch with second hand

Grid paper (provided as blackline masters)

Transparent grids (optional)

Paper cutouts of hexagons (optional)

Colored pencils (optional)

Graphing calculator linking cable (optional)

Overhead graphing calculator (optional)

Mathematics in the Unit

- Understand that variables in a situation are those quantities that change, such as time, temperature, feelings, a TV show's popularity, distance traveled, and speed.
- Understand that patterns describe a regular or predictable change in data.
- Search for patterns of change that show relationships among the variables.
- Select an appropriate range of values for the variables.
- Create tables, graphs, and simple symbolic rules that describe the patterns of change.
- Understand the relationships among forms of representation—words, tables, graphs, and symbolic rules.
- Make decisions using tables, graphs, and rules.
- Use a graphing calculator for making tables and graphs to find information about a situation.

© Prentice-Hall, Inc.

Connections to Other Units

The ideas in *Variables and Patterns* build on and connect to several big ideas in other Connected Mathematics units.

Big Idea	Prior Work	Future Work
collecting, organizing, and representing data	gathering data by conducting trials of an experiment or game; organizing data in tables and graphs in order to look for patterns and relationships (*Data About Us; How Likely Is It?*)	analyzing patterns to develop concepts of surface area and volume (*Filling and Wrapping*); studying data to develop the concept of linear, exponential, and quadratic functions (*Moving Straight Ahead; Growing, Growing, Growing; Frogs, Fleas, and Painted Cubes*); gathering and analyzing data about populations (*Samples and Populations*)
identifying patterns and extreme values in data organized in graphs or tables; making inferences about situations based on such information	identifying patterns in number and geometry (*Prime Time; Shapes and Designs*); analyzing maximum and minimum values in measurement (*Covering and Surrounding*)	understanding relationships between edge lengths and surface area and volume of three-dimensional figures (*Filling and Wrapping*); identifying maximum and minimum values for a mathematical model or equation (*Thinking with Mathematical Models; Frogs, Fleas, and Painted Cubes*)
analyzing a pattern or relationship in a graph or table to identify variables and interpret the relationship between the variables	organizing, displaying, and interpreting data in one- and two-dimensional graphs and tables (*Data About Us*); constructing graphs of the relationship between the dimensions and area of a rectangle when the perimeter is held constant and between the dimensions and perimeter when the area is held constant (*Covering and Surrounding*)	extending tables and graphs to include negative coordinates and quantities (*Accentuate the Negative*); formalizing understandings of linear equations in $y = mx + b$ form (Moving Straight Ahead); studying and developing mathematical models (*Thinking with Mathematical Models*); identifying and studying nonlinear patterns of growth (*Growing, Growing, Growing; Frogs, Fleas, and Painted Cubes*)
analyzing linear relationships and expressing them as written and symbolic rules	developing operation algorithms for fractions, decimals, and percents (*Bits and Pieces II*); programming a computer in Logo to construct two-dimensional geometric shapes (*Shapes and Designs*)	expressing linear relationships in $y = mx + b$ form (*Moving Straight Ahead*); describing situations with linear models or equations (*Thinking with Mathematical Models*); developing strategies for expressing linear relationships in symbols and for solving linear equations (*Say It with Symbols*)
using graphing calculators to organize and represent data and to analyze linear relationships	producing geometric figures with Logo (*Shapes and Designs*)	using graphing calculators to graph and compare lines (*Moving Straight Ahead*); using graphing calculators to develop and study mathematical models (*Thinking with Mathematical Models*); performing isometries in two dimensions (*Kaleidoscopes, Hubcaps, and Mirrors*)

© Prentice-Hall, Inc.

Lesson Planner

Investigation 1: Variables and Coordinate Graphs

Mathematical and Problem-Solving Goals

■ To collect data from an experiment and then make a table and a graph to organize and represent the data

■ To search for explanations for patterns and variations in data

■ To understand that a variable is a quantity that changes and to recognize variables in the real world

■ To understand that in order to make a graph that shows the relationship between two variables, you need to identify the two variables, choose an axis for each, and select an appropriate scale for each axis

■ To interpret information given in a graph

Problems in this Investigation

Problem 1.1: Preparing for a Bicycle Tour *(pages 5–7)*

Problem 1.2: Making Graphs *(pages 7–9)*

Resource Options for Planning

	Suggested Pacing	Assignment Guide (ACE questions)	Materials for Students	Resources for Teachers
Investigation 1	3 days total	Exercises are in Student Edition, pp. 10–16	■ graphing calculators	■ Additional Practice, Investigation 1 (TG, pp. 132–133)
Problem 1.1	1 day	5	■ clock or watch with second hand	■ Transparency 1.1 (TG, p. 101) *
Problem 1.2	2 days	1–4, 6–8	■ grid paper ■ transparent grids *	■ Transparency 1.2A (TG, p. 102) * ■ Transparency 1.2B (TG, p. 103) * ■ transparent grid * ■ Grid paper BLM (TG, p. 129)
Mathematical Reflections		MR 1, 2	■ journal	

* optional materials

© Prentice-Hall, Inc.

Lesson Planner

Investigation 2: Graphing Change

Mathematical and Problem-Solving Goals

- To make sense of data given in the form of a table or a graph
- To read a narrative of a situation that changes over time and make a table and graph that represent these changes
- To read data given in a table and make a graph from the table
- To read data given in a graph and make a table from the graph
- To compare tables, graphs, and narratives and understand the advantages and disadvantages of each form of representation

Problems in this Investigation

Problem 2.1: Day 1: Philadelphia to Atlantic City *(pages 18–19)*

Problem 2.2: Day 2: Atlantic City to Lewes *(pages 20–21)*

Problem 2.3: Day 3: Lewes to Chincoteague Island *(pages 22–23)*

Problem 2.4: Day 4: Chincoteague Island to Norfolk *(pages 23–24)*

Problem 2.5: Day 5: Norfolk to Williamsburg *(pages 24–25)*

Resource Options for Planning

	Suggested Pacing	Assignment Guide (ACE questions)	Materials for Students	Resources for Teachers
Investigation 2	5 days total	Exercises are in Student Edition, pp. 26–34	■ graphing calculators ■ grid paper	■ Additional Practice, Investigation 2 (TG, pp. 134–135) ■ Grid paper BLM (TG, p. 129)
Problem 2.1	1 day	9		■ Transparency 2.1A (TG, p. 104) * ■ Transparency 2.1B (TG, p. 105) *
Problem 2.2	1 day	1, 10, 11		■ Transparency 2.2A (TG, p. 106) * ■ Transparency 2.2B (TG, p. 107) * ■ Transparency 2.2C (TG, p. 108) *
Problem 2.3	1 day	2, 8		■ Transparency 2.3 (TG, p. 109) *
Problem 2.4	1 day	3, 5–7		■ Transparency 2.4 (TG, p. 110) *
Problem 2.5	1 day	4, 12, 13	■ paper cutouts of hexagons *	■ Transparency 2.5 (TG, p. 11) *
Mathematical Reflections		MR 1–3	■ journal	

* optional materials

© Prentice-Hall, Inc.

Investigation 3: Analyzing Graphs and Tables

Mathematical and Problem-Solving Goals

■ To change the form of representation of data from tables to graphs and vice versa

■ To search for patterns of change

■ To describe situations that change in predictable ways with rules in words for predicting the change

■ To compare forms of representation of data

Problems in this Investigation

Problem 3.1: Renting Bicycles *(pages 37–38)*

Problem 3.2: Finding Customers *(pages 38–39)*

Problem 3.3: Predicting Profit *(pages 39–40)*

Problem 3.4: Paying Bills and Counting Profits *(pages 40–41)*

Resource Options for Planning

	Suggested Pacing	Assignment Guide (ACE questions)	Materials for Students	Resources for Teachers
Investigation 3	4 days total	Exercises are in Student Edition, pp. 42–47	■ graphing calculators ■ grid paper	■ Additional Practice, Investigation 3 (TG, pp. 136–137) ■ Grid paper BLM (TG, p. 129)
Problem 3.1	1 day	3, 4		■ Transparency 3.1A (TG, p. 112) * ■ Transparency 3.1B (TG, p. 113) *
Problem 3.2	1 day	7–9		■ Transparency 3.2 (TG, p. 114) *
Problem 3.3	1 day	5, 6		■ Transparency 3.3 (TG, p. 115) *
Problem 3.4	1 day	1, 2, 10		■ Transparency 3.4A (TG, p. 116) * ■ Transparency 3.4B (TG, p. 117) *
Mathematical Reflections		MR 1–4	■ Journal	

* optional materials

© Prentice-Hall, Inc.

Lesson Planner

Investigation 4: Patterns and Rules

Mathematical and Problem-Solving Goals

■ To understand the relationship between rate, time, and distance

■ To represent information regarding rates in tables and graphs and to use tables and graphs to compare rates

■ To search for patterns of predictable change

■ To learn to express in words and symbols situations that change in predictable ways

Problems in this Investigation

Problem 4.1: Heading Home *(pages 50–51)*

Problem 4.2: Changing Speeds *(pages 51–52)*

Problem 4.3: Calculating Costs and Profits *(pages 52–53)*

Resource Options for Planning

	Suggested Pacing	Assignment Guide (ACE questions)	Materials for Students	Resources for Teachers
Investigation 4	3 days total	Exercises are in Student Edition, pp. 54–59	■ graphing calculator ■ grid paper	■ Additional Practice, Investigation 4 (TG, p. 138) ■ Grid paper BLM (TG, p. 129)
Problem 4.1	1 day	10, 13		■ Transparency 4.1A (TG, p. 118) * ■ Transparency 4.1B (TG, p. 119) *
Problem 4.2	1 day	1, 2, 8, 9		■ Transparency 4.2A (TG, p. 120) * ■ Transparency 4.2B (TG, p. 121) * ■ Transparency 4.2C (TG, p. 122) *
Problem 4.3	1 day	3–7, 11, 12, 14		■ Transparency 4.3A (TG, p. 123) * ■ Transparency 4.3B (TG, p. 124) *
Mathematical Reflections		MR 1, 2	■ journal	

* optional materials

© Prentice-Hall, Inc.

Lesson Planner

Investigation 5: Using a Graphing Calculator

Mathematical and Problem-Solving Goals

- To use a rule to generate a table or graph on the graphing calculator
- To use a graphing calculator to compare the tables and graphs of various rules; in particular, to decide whether a given rule defines a straight-line (linear) function by examining graphs

Problems in this Investigation

Problem 5.1: Graphing on a Calculator *(pages 61–63)*

Problem 5.2: Making Tables on a Calculator *(page 63)*

Resource Options for Planning

	Suggested Pacing	Assignment Guide (ACE questions)	Materials for Students	Resources for Teachers
Investigation 5	3 days total	Exercises are in Student Edition, pp. 64–67	■ graphing calculators ■ grid paper	■ Additional Practice, Investigation 5 (TG, p. 139) ■ Grid paper BLM (TG, p. 129) ■ overhead graphing calculator * ■ linking software to allow printing of calculator screens and copying features of calculator screens *
Problem 5.1	1 day	3, 4, 6	■ Labsheet 5.1 (2 per group) *	■ Transparency 5.1 (TG, p. 125) * ■ Labsheet 5.1 BLM (TG, p. 100) *
Problem 5.2	2 day	1, 2, 5, 7		■ Transparency 5.2 (TG, p. 126) *
Mathematical Reflections		MR 1–3	■ journal	

* optional materials

© Prentice-Hall, Inc.

Unit Organizer

Stretching and Shrinking

Pacing Options

Investigations and Assessments	Class Time (days)
1 Enlarging Figures (SE, pp. 5–13)	2
2 Similar Figures (SE, pp. 14–27)	4
Check-Up (TG, pp. 90–92)	1/2
3 Patterns of Similar Figures (SE, pp. 28–40)	3
Quiz A (TG, pp. 93–95)	1
4 Using Similarity (SE, pp. 41–58)	4
Quiz B (TG, pp. 96–98)	1
5 Similar Triangles (SE, pp. 59–74)	3
6 Stretching and Shrinking with a Computer (SE, pp. 75–84)	2
Looking Back and Looking Ahead: Unit Reflections (SE, pp. 86–87)	1
Unit Test (TG, pp. 103–106)	1
Self-Assessment (TG, p. 110)	take home
Unit Project (SE, p. 85, optional)	1

Teacher's Guide and Ancillary Resources

Assessment Resources (pp. 87–122)

Blackline Masters (pp. 123–169)

Additional Practice (pp. 171–180)

 Assessment and Additional Practice

Essential Vocabulary

compare

corresponds, corresponding

image

ratio

scale, scale factor

similar

Prerequisite Units

Shapes and Designs (Geometry, Measurement)

NCTM Principles and Standards 2000

Content Standard: Geometry, Measurement

Process Standards: Problem Solving, Reasoning and Proof, Communication, Connections, and Representation

Materials

Graphing calculators

Shapes A, B, C, D, G, I, J, K, L, O, P, R, and T from the ShapeSet™ or 4 copies of each cut from Labsheet 3.2 (1 set per student)

No. 16 (3 inch) rubber bands (2 per student)

State or local maps (optional)

Mirrors (1 per student or group)

Transparent centimeter and half-centimeter grids (optional; copy the grids onto transparency film)

Macintosh computer with Turtle Math software (optional; 1 for every 2–4 students)

Angle rulers (1 per 2–4 students)

Tools for measuring longer distances, such as tape measures, string, or sticks cut to 1 meter

$8\frac{1}{2}$" by 11", 11" by 14", and 11" by 17" paper (optional)

Mathematics in the Unit

- Enlarge figures using rubber-band stretchers and coordinate plotting.
- Informally visualize and identify similar and distorted transformations.
- Recognize that lengths between similar figures change by a constant scale factor.
- Build larger, similar shapes from a basic shape and divide a basic shape into smaller, similar shapes.
- Recognize the relationship between similarity and equivalent fractions.
- Learn the effect of scale factor on length ratios and area ratios.
- Recognize that triangles with equal corresponding sides are similar.
- Recognize that rectangles with equivalent ratios of corresponding sides are similar.
- Find and use scale factors to find unknown lengths.
- Collect examples of figures and search for patterns.
- Use the concept of similarity to solve real-world problems.
- Draw or construct counterexamples to explore similarity transformations.
- Make connections between algebra and geometry.
- Use geometry software to explore similarity transformations.

© Prentice-Hall, Inc.

Connections to Other Units

The ideas in *Stretching and Shrinking* build on and connect to several big ideas in other Connected Mathematics units.

Big Idea	Prior Work	Future Work
enlarging and shrinking plane figures	finding angle measures, lengths, and areas of plane geometric figures *(Shapes and Designs; Covering and Surrounding)*	scaling quantities, objects, and shapes up and down *(Comparing and Scaling; Filling and Wrapping; Data Around Us)*
identifying the corresponding parts of similar figures	developing and applying concepts of vertex, angle, angle measure, side, and side length *(Shapes and Designs; Covering and Surrounding)*	analyzing how two-dimensional shapes are affected by different isometries; generating isometric transformations *(Kaleidoscopes, Hubcaps, and Mirrors)*
describing and producing transformations of plane figures	developing computer programs to construct two-dimensional shapes *(Shapes and Designs)*; developing strategies for representing three-dimensional objects in two dimensions *(Ruins of Montarek)*; using symbols to communicate operations *(Variables and Patterns)*	finding the equation of a line *(Moving Straight Ahead)*; expressing linear relationships with symbols; determining whether linear expressions are equivalent *(Say It with Symbols)*; writing directions for isometries in two dimensions *(Kaleidoscopes, Hubcaps, and Mirrors)*
analyzing scale factors between figures; applying scale factors to solve two-dimensional geometric problems	using factors and multiples *(Prime Time)*; measuring two-dimensional figures *(Covering and Surrounding)*; using ratios in fraction form *(Bits and Pieces I; Bits and Pieces II)*; using maps *(Variables and Patterns)*	scaling and comparing figures and quantities *(Comparing and Scaling; Data Around Us)*; using slope to solve problems involving linear relationships *(Moving Straight Ahead)*
applying properties of similar figures	exploring properties of two-dimensional shapes; finding areas, perimeters, and side lengths of shapes *(Shapes and Designs; Covering and Surrounding)*	exploring ratios and proportional relationships *(Comparing and Scaling)*; developing the concept of slope *(Moving Straight Ahead)*
using the computer program Turtle Math to generate similar figures and to apply properties of similar figures	writing Logo programs to produce geometric shapes with specified properties *(Shapes and Designs)*	using a graphing calculator to apply mathematical models to problem situations *(Thinking with Mathematical Models)*

© Prentice-Hall, Inc.

Investigation 1: Enlarging Figures

Mathematical and Problem-Solving Goals

- To make enlargements of simple figures with a rubber-band stretcher
- To describe in an intuitive way what the word similar means
- To consider relationships between lengths and between angles in simple, similar figures

Problems in this Investigation

Problem 1.1: Stretching a Figure *(pages 5–8)*

Resource Options for Planning

	Suggested Pacing	Assignment Guide (ACE questions)	Materials for Students	Resources for Teachers
Investigation 1	2 days total	Exercises are in Student Edition, pp. 9–12	■ graphing calculators	■ Additional Practice, Investigation 1 (TG, p. 172)
Problem 1.1	2 days	1–7	■ Labsheet 1.1A or 1.1B (1 per student) ■ Labsheet 1.2A or 1.2B (1 per student) ■ transparent centimeter and half-centimeter grids * ■ no. 16 (3 inch) rubber bands (2 per student) ■ masking tape ■ blank sheets of paper (1 per student)	■ Transparency 1.1A (TG, p. 135) * ■ Transparency 1.1B (TG, p. 136) * ■ chart paper * ■ 2 rubber bands ■ Labsheet 1.1A or 1.1B BLM (TG, pp. 124–125) ■ Labsheet 1.2A or 1.2B BLM (TG, pp. 126–127) ■ Centimeter grid BLM (TG, p. 165) ■ Half-centimeter grid BLM (TG, p. 164)
Mathematical Reflections		MR 1, 2	■ journal	

* optional materials

© Prentice-Hall, Inc.

Lesson Planner

Investigation 2: Similar Figures

Mathematical and Problem-Solving Goals

- To review locating points in a coordinate system
- To graph figures using algebraic rules
- To predict how figures on a coordinate system are affected by a given rule
- To learn that corresponding angles of similar figures are equal and that corresponding sides grow by the same factor
- To compare lengths and angles in similar and nonsimilar figures informally
- To experiment with examples and counterexamples of similar shapes

Problems in this Investigation

Problem 2.1: Drawing Wumps *(pages 15–18)*

Problem 2.2: Nosing Around *(pages 18–20)*

Problem 2.3: Making Wump Hats *(page 21)*

Resource Options for Planning

	Suggested Pacing	Assignment Guide (ACE questions)	Materials for Students	Resources for Teachers
Investigation 2	4 days total	Exercises are in Student Edition, pp. 22–26	■ graphing calculators ■ angle rulers (1 per student) * ■ centimeter grid paper	■ Additional Practice, Investigation 2 (TG, p. 173) ■ transparent centimeter grids ■ transparent half-centimeter grids ■ Centimeter grid BLM (TG, p. 165) ■ Half-centimeter grid BLM (TG, p. 164)
Problem 2.1	1 day	1, 3, 11–13	■ Labsheet 2.1A (1 per student) ■ Labsheet 2.1B (3 per student) ■ transparent grids *	■ Transparency 2.1A (TG, p. 137) * ■ Transparency 2.1B (TG, p. 138) * ■ Transparency 2.1C (TG, p. 139) * ■ Transparency 2.1D (TG, p. 140) * ■ Labsheets 2.1A and 2.1B BLM (TG, pp. 128–129) *
Problem 2.2	1 day	2, 4, 5		■ Transparency 2.2A (TG, p. 141) * ■ Transparency 2.2B (TG, p. 142) *
Problem 2.3	2 days	6–10, 14	■ Labsheets 2.3A and 2.3B (1 each per student)	■ Transparency 2.3A (TG, p. 143) * ■ Transparency 2.3B (TG, p. 144) * ■ Labsheets 2.3A and 2.3B BLM (TG, pp. 143–144)
Mathematical Reflections		MR 1–3	■ journal	

* optional materials

© Prentice-Hall, Inc.

Lesson Planner

Investigation 3: Patterns of Similar Figures

Mathematical and Problem-Solving Goals

- To recognize similar figures and to be able to tell why they are similar
- To understand that any two similar figures are related by a scale factor, which is the ratio of their corresponding sizes
- To build a larger, similar shape from copies of a basic shape (a rep-tile)
- To find rep-tiles by dividing a large shape into smaller, similar shapes
- To understand that the sides and perimeters of similar figures grow by a scale factor and that the areas grow by the square of the scale factor
- To find a missing measurement in a pair of similar figures
- To recognize that triangles with equal corresponding angles are similar

Problems in this Investigation

Problem 3.1: Identifying Similar Figures *(pages 28–29)*
Problem 3.2: Building with Rep-tiles *(pages 29–31)*
Problem 3.3: Subdividing to Find Rep-tiles *(pages 31–32)*

Resource Options for Planning

	Suggested Pacing	Assignment Guide (ACE questions)	Materials for Students	Resources for Teachers
Investigation 3	3 days total	Exercises are in Student Edition, pp. 31–36	■ graphing calculators ■ angle rulers (1 per group) * ■ rulers (1 per group) *	■ Grid paper BLM (TG, p. 130) ■ cubes ■ transparent grid ■ Additional Practice, Investigation 3 (TG, pp. 174–175)
Problem 3.1	1 day	1–7, 16, 17	■ Labsheet 3.1 (1 per group) ■ transparent centimeter and half-centimeter grids * ■ transparency markers *	■ Transparency 3.1A (TG, p. 145) * ■ Labsheet 3.1 BLM (TG, p. 132) ■ Transparency 3.1B (TG, p. 146) * ■ transparency of Labsheet 3.1 * ■ Centimeter grid BLM (TG, p. 165) ■ Half-centimeter grid BLM (TG, p. 164) ■ Transparency 3.ACE (TG, p. 149) *
Problem 3.2	1 day	11–14, 18, 19	■ figures A, B, C, D, G, I, J, K, L, O, P, R, and T from the ShapeSet™ or 4 copies of each cut from Labsheet 3.2 (1 set per student)	■ Transparency 3.2 (TG, p. 147) * ■ Labsheet 3.2 BLM (TG, p. 133) ■ transparency of Labsheet 3.2 * ■ large U.S. map * ■ ShapeSet™ or transparencies of the shapes from Labsheet 3.2
Problem 3.3	1 day	8–10, 15, 20	■ Labsheet 3.3 (1 per student) ■ scissors *	■ Transparency 3.3 (TG, p. 148) * ■ transparency of Labsheet 3.3 * ■ Labsheet 3.3 BLM (TG, p. 134)
Mathematical Reflections		MR 1–4	■ journal	

* optional materials

© Prentice-Hall, Inc.

Lesson Planner

Investigation 4: Using Similarity

Mathematical and Problem-Solving Goals

- To use the defintion of similarity to recognize when figures are similar
- To determine the scale factor between similar figures to find the lengths of corresponding sides
- To find a missing measurement in a pair of similar figures
- To use the relationship between scale factor and area to find the area of a figure that is similar to a figure of a known area
- To solve problems that involve scaling up and down

Problems in this Investigation

Problem 4.1: Using Similarity to Solve a Mystery *(pages 41–42)*

Problem 4.2: Scaling Up *(page 43)*

Problem 4.3: Making Copies *(page 44)*

Problem 4.4: Using Map Scales *(pages 45–46)*

Resource Options for Planning

	Suggested Pacing	Assignment Guide (ACE questions)	Materials for Students	Resources for Teachers
Investigation 4	4 days total	Exercises are in Student Edition, pp. 47–57	■ graphing calculators ■ rulers (1 per pair)	■ Additional Practice, Investigation 4 (TG, pp. 176–177)
Problem 4.1	1 day	1–7, 16–20		■ Transparency 4.1 (TG, p. 150) *
Problem 4.2	1 day	8, 9, 15	■ centimeter and half-centimeter grid paper *	■ Transparency 4.2 (TG, p. 151) * ■ Centimeter grid BLM (TG, p. 165) ■ Half-centimeter grid BLM (TG, p. 164)
Problem 4.3	1 day	10–14, 21, 22	■ grid paper *	■ Transparency 4.3 (TG, p. 152) * ■ $8\frac{1}{2}$" by 11", 11" by 14", and 11" by 17 " sheets of paper (1 of each) *
Problem 4.4 **Mathematical Reflections**	1 day	23–31 MR 1–4	■ state or local maps (1 per group) * ■ journal	■ Transparency 4.4 (TG, p. 153) *

* optional materials

© Prentice-Hall, Inc.

Lesson Planner

Investigation 5: Similar Triangles

Mathematical and Problem-Solving Goals

■ To recognize similar figures in the real world

■ To find a missing measurement in a pair of similar figures

■ To apply what has been learned about similar figures to solve real-world problems

■ To collect data, analyze it, and draw reasoned conclusions from it

Problems in this Investigation

Problem 5.1: Using Shadows to Find Heights *(pages 59–61)*

Problem 5.2: Using Mirrors to Find Heights *(pages 61–62)*

Problem 5.3: Using Similar Triangles to Find Distances *(page 63)*

Resource Options for Planning

	Suggested Pacing	Assignment Guide (ACE questions)	Materials for Students	Resources for Teachers
Investigation 5	3 days total	Exercises are in Student Edition, pp. 64–73	■ graphing calculators ■ metersticks (1 per student or group)	■ Additional Practice, Investigation 5 (TG, pp. 178–179)
Problem 5.1	1 day	1–4, 7, 13		■ Transparency 5.1 (TG, p. 154) *
Problem 5.2	1 day	5, 6, 8, 10, 11, 12, 14	■ mirrors (1 per student or group)	■ Transparency 5.2 (TG, p. 155) *
Problem 5.3	1 day	9, 15, 16	■ tools for measuring longer distances, such as tape measures, string, or sticks cut to 1 meter	■ Transparency 5.3 (TG, p. 156) *
Mathematical Reflections		MR 1–3	■ journal	

* optional materials

© Prentice-Hall, Inc.

Lesson Planner

Investigation 6: Stretching and Shrinking with a Computer

Mathematical and Problem-Solving Goals

- To continue to make decisions about whether figures are similar based upon constant angle measurements and ratios between two sides of the same figure

- To continue to build understanding of angles as measures of rotation

- To solve problems involving scaling and its effects on side lengths and area

- To manipulate a figure visually by shrinking it to zero length and width and then changing its orientation (as the scale factor becomes negative)

Problems in this Investigation

Problem 6.1: Drawing Similar Figures with a Computer *(pages 75–78)*

Problem 6.2: Stretching and Shrinking Flags *(pages 79–80)*

Resource Options for Planning

	Suggested Pacing	Assignment Guide (ACE questions)	Materials for Students	Resources for Teachers
Investigation 6	2 days total	Exercises are in Student Edition, pp. 81–83	■ graphing calculators ■ Macintosh computers * ■ Turtle Math software *	■ Additional Practice, Investigation 6 (TG, p. 180) ■ overhead computer display *
Problem 6.1	1 day	1	■ angle rulers (1 per 2–4 students)	■ Transparency 6.1A (TG, p. 157) * ■ Transparency 6.1B (TG, p. 158) * ■ Transparency 6.1C (TG, p. 159) * ■ Transparency 6.1D (TG, p. 160) *
Problem 6.2 **Mathematical Reflections**	1 day	2, 3 MR 1–3	■ grid paper * ■ transparent grids * ■ journal	■ Transparency 6.2 (TG, p. 161) * ■ Grid paper BLM (TG, p. 165)

* optional materials

© Prentice-Hall, Inc.

Comparing and Scaling

Pacing Options

Investigations and Assessments	Class Time (days)
1 Making Comparisons (SE, pp. 5–15)	4
2 Comparing by Finding Percents (SE, pp. 16–25)	2
Check-Up 1 (TG, pp. 86–87)	1/2
3 Comparing by Using Ratios (SE, pp. 26–36)	3
4 Comparing by Finding Rates (SE, pp. 37–51)	4
Check-Up 2 (TG, p. 88)	1/2
Quiz (TG, pp. 89–90)	1
5 Estimating Populations and Population Densities (SE, pp. 52–64)	5
6 Choosing Strategies (SE, pp. 65–81)	3
Looking Back and Looking Ahead: Unit Reflections (SE, pp. 84–86)	1
Unit Test (TG, pp. 96–97)	1
Self-Assessment (TG, p. 101)	take home
Unit Project (SE, pp. 82–83, optional)	2–3

Teacher's Guide and Ancillary Resources

Assessment Resources (pp. 85–116)

Blackline Masters (pp. 117–150)

Additional Practice (pp. 151–159)

 Assessment and
Additional Practice

Essential Vocabulary

population density

rate

ratio

scale, scaling

unit rate

Prerequisite Units

Shapes and Designs (Geometry, Measurement)

Stretching and Shrinking (Geometry, Measurement)

NCTM Principles and Standards 2000

Content Standard: Number and Operations, Algebra

Process Standards: Problem Solving, Reasoning and Proof, Communication, Connections, and Representation

Materials

Graphing calculators

Containers (large enough so students can mix contents) of 300–800 white beans, with lid

Scoops for sampling (optional)

Marker

Large sheets of paper

Centimeter and inch grid paper (provided as BLM)

Advertisements containing comparisions (optional)

Can of orange juice concentrate and pitcher (optional)

News article that reports an estimate of crowd size (optional)

Mathematics in the Unit

- Use informal language to ask comparison questions, such as:

  "What fraction of the class is going to the picnic?"

  "What percent of the girls play basketball?"

  "Which model of car has the best fuel economy?"

- Decide when the most informative comparison is the difference between two quantities and when it is ratios between pairs of quantities.

- Develop the ability to make judgments about rounding data to estimate ratio comparisons.

- Find equivalent ratios to make more accurate and insightful comparisons.

- Scale a ratio or fraction up or down so that a larger or smaller object or population has the same relative characteristics as the original.

- Represent data in tables and graphs.

- Apply proportional reasoning to situations in which capture-tag-recapture methods are appropriate for estimating population counts.

- Set up and solve proportions that arise in applications.

- Look for patterns in tables that will allow predictions.

- Connect unit rates with a rule describing the situation.

- Begin to recognize that constant growth in a table will give a straight-line graph.

- Use rates to describe population and traffic density.

© Prentice-Hall, Inc.

Connections to Other Units

The ideas in *Comparing and Scaling* build on and connect to several big ideas in other Connected Mathematics units.

Big Idea	Prior Work	Future Work
exploring proportional relationships between quantities	exploring and applying rational number concepts *(Bits and Pieces I; Bits and Pieces II)*	calculating and applying slope in equations of the form $y = mx + b$ *(Moving Straight Ahead; Thinking with Mathematical Models; Say It with Symbols)*
using percents to create a common scale for comparing two data sets (i.e., using percents allows you to express all quantities as values "out of 100")	defining percent as "out of 100"; connecting fractions, decimals, and percents *(Bits and Pieces I; Bits and Pieces II)*	making comparisons between groups of different sizes *(Data Around Us; Samples and Populations)*
interpreting fractions as ratios, as rates, or as comparisons of a part to the whole	interpreting fractions as part-to-whole comparisons; adding, subtracting, multiplying, and dividing fractions *(Bits and Pieces II; How Likely Is It?)*	expressing and applying probabilities as fractions *(What Do You Expect?)*; determining whether two algebraic expressions are equivalent *(Say It with Symbols)*
scaling ratios up or down	comparing and subdividing similar figures to determine scale factors *(Stretching and Shrinking)*	scaling up rectangular prisms *(Filling and Wrapping)*
comparing quantities using ratios, rates, or percents	comparing fractions, decimals, and percents *(Bits and Pieces I; Bits and Pieces II)*; comparing data sets *(Data About Us)*	comparing probabilities *(What Do You Expect?; Samples and Populations)*; comparing data sets *(Data Around Us)*
developing techniques to estimate population densities and other quantities	making inferences about quantities and populations based on experimental or theoretical probabilities *(How Likely Is It?)*	estimating with and comparing large numbers *(Data Around Us)*; developing benchmarks and skills for estimating irrational numbers *(Looking for Pythagoras)*; estimating populations *(Samples and Populations)*

© Prentice-Hall, Inc.

Lesson Planner

Investigation 1: Making Comparisons

Mathematical and Problem-Solving Goals

- To explore several ways to make comparisons

- To begin to understand how to determine when comparisons can be made using multiplication or division versus addition or subtraction

- To begin to develop ways to use ratios, fractions, rates, and unit rates to answer questions involving proportional reasoning

Problems in this Investigation

Problem 1.1: Writing Ads *(pages 5–6)*

Problem 1.2: Targeting an Audience *(pages 7–8)*

Problem 1.3: Getting the Message Across *(pages 8–9)*

Resource Options for Planning

	Suggested Pacing	Assignment Guide (ACE questions)	Materials for Students	Resources for Teachers
Investigation 1	4 days total	Exercises are in Student Edition, pp. 10–14	■ graphing calculators	■ Additional Practice, Investigation 1 (TG, p. 172)
Problem 1.1	1 day	6–11		■ Transparency 1.1 (TG, p. 124) * ■ advertisements containing comparisons *
Problem 1.2	1 day	1–5, 13		■ Transparency 1.2A (TG, p. 125) * ■ Transparency 1.2B (TG, p. 126) *
Problem 1.3 **Mathematical Reflections**	2 days	12, 14 MR 1, 2	■ large sheets of paper (1 per group) * ■ journal	■ Transparency 1.3 (TG, p. 127) *

* optional materials

© Prentice-Hall, Inc.

Investigation 2: Comparing by Finding Percents

Mathematical and Problem-Solving Goals

- To further develop the ability to make sensible comparisons of data using ratios, fractions, and decimal rates, with a focus on percents
- To develop the ability to make judgments about rounding data to estimate ratio comparisons
- To observe what is common about situations that call for a certain type of ratio comparison

Problems in this Investigation

Problem 2.1: Comparing Leisure Activities *(pages 17–18)*

Problem 2.2: Comparing Your Class to the Nation *(pages 18–19)*

Resource Options for Planning

	Suggested Pacing	Assignment Guide (ACE questions)	Materials for Students	Resources for Teachers
Investigation 2	2 days total	Exercises are in Student Edition, pp. 20–24	■ graphing calculators	■ Additional Practice, Investigation 2 (TG, p. 173)
Problem 2.1	1 day	1–8, 17–22	■ centimeter grid paper *	■ Transparency 2.1 (TG, p. 128) * ■ Centimeter Grid paper BLM (TG, p. 149) *
Problem 2.2	1 day	9–16, 23–26		■ Transparency 2.2 (TG, p. 129) *
Mathematical Reflections		MR 1–5	■ journal	

* optional materials

© Prentice-Hall, Inc.

Investigation 3: Comparing by Using Ratios

Mathematical and Problem-Solving Goals

- To recognize situations in which ratios are a useful form of comparison

- To form, label, and interpret ratios from numbers given or implied in a situation

- To explore several informal strategies for solving scaling problems involving ratios (which is equivalent to solving proportions)

Problems in this Investigation

Problem 3.1: Mixing Juice *(pages 27–28)*

Problem 3.2: Helping the Cook *(page 29)*

Problem 3.3: Sharing Pizza *(page 30)*

Resource Options for Planning

	Suggested Pacing	Assignment Guide (ACE questions)	Materials for Students	Resources for Teachers
Investigation 3	3 days total	Exercises are in Student Edition, pp. 31–35	■ graphing calculators ■ centimeter grid paper *	■ Additional Practice, Investigation 3 (TG, pp. 174–175) ■ overhead graphing calculator * ■ Centimeter grid paper BLM (TG, p. 149)*
Problem 3.1	1 day	1, 2, 9–12	■ orange and white chips or squares of paper (about 25 orange and 100 white per group) *	■ Transparency 3.1 (TG, p. 130) * ■ can of orange juice concentrate and pitcher *
Problem 3.2	1 day	3, 5, 6, 13–24		■ Transparency 3.2 (TG, p. 131) *
Problem 3.3	1 day	4, 7, 8, 25		■ Transparency 3.3 (TG, p. 132) *
Mathematical Reflections		MR 1–4	■ journal	

* optional materials

© Prentice-Hall, Inc.

Investigation 4: Comparing by Finding Rates

Mathematical and Problem-Solving Goals

- To find unit rates
- To represent data in tables and graphs
- To look for patterns in tables in order to make predictions beyond the tables
- To connect unit rates with the rule describing a situation
- To begin to recognize that constant growth in a table will give a straight line graph
- To find the missing value in a proportion

Problems in this Investigation

Problem 4.1: Comparing Fuel Economy *(pages 38–39)*

Problem 4.2: Using Unit Rates *(pages 40–41)*

Problem 4.3: Solving Problems with Rates *(page 42)*

Problem 4.4: Buying Beads *(page 43)*

Resource Options for Planning

	Suggested Pacing	Assignment Guide (ACE questions)	Materials for Students	Resources for Teachers
Investigation 4	4 days total	Exercises are in Student Edition, pp. 44–50	■ graphing calculators	■ Additional Practice, Investigation 4 (TG, pp. 176–177)
Problem 4.1	1 day	4, 5		■ Transparency 4.1 (TG, p. 133) *
Problem 4.2	1 day	1, 6, 10, 11, 17–20	■ centimeter grid paper	■ Transparency 4.2 (TG, p. 134) * ■ Centimeter grid paper BLM (TG, p. 149)
Problem 4.3	1 day	2, 3, 8, 9, 21	■ centimeter grid paper ■ transparencies of centimeter grid paper and transparency markers *	■ Transparency 4.3 (TG, p. 135) * ■ Centimeter grid paper BLM (TG, p. 149)
Problem 4.4	1 day	7, 12–16, 22, 23		■ Transparency 4.4 (TG, p. 136) *
Mathematical Reflections		MR 1–5	■ journal	

* optional materials

© Prentice-Hall, Inc.

Lesson Planner

Investigation 5: Estimating Populations and Population Densities

Mathematical and Problem-Solving Goals

■ To use geometric scaling to estimate population counts

■ To apply proportional reasoning to situations in which capture-tag-recapture methods are appropriate for estimating population counts

■ To use ratios and scaling up or down (finding equivalent ratios) to find the missing value in a proportion

■ To use rates to describe population and traffic density (space per person or car)

Problems in this Investigation

Problem 5.1: Estimating the Size of a Crowd *(pages 52–53)*

Problem 5.2: Estimating a Deer Population *(page 54)*

Problem 5.3: Finding Population Densities *(pages 55–56)*

Problem 5.4: Comparing the Dakotas *(page 57)*

Problem 5.5: Predicting Traffic Jams *(page 58)*

Resource Options for Planning

	Suggested Pacing	Assignment Guide (ACE questions)	Materials for Students	Resources for Teachers
Investigation 5	5 days total	Exercises are in Student Edition, pp. 59–63	■ graphing calculators	■ Additional Practice, Investigation 5 (TG, pp. 178–179)
Problem 5.1	1 day	3, 10	■ transparency of centimeter grid paper ■ transparency of inch grid paper	■ Transparency 5.1 (TG, p. 137) * ■ Centimeter grid paper BLM (TG, p. 149) ■ Inch grid paper BLM (TG, p. 150) ■ news articles that report an estimate of crowd size *
Problem 5.2	1 day	1, 2, 4, 13, 14	■ containers (large enough so students can mix contents) of 300–800 white beans, with lid (1 per group) ■ markers (1 per group) ■ scoops for sampling (1 per group) *	■ Transparency 5.2 (TG, p. 138) *
Problem 5.3	1 day	5, 7, 8		■ Transparency 5.3A (TG, p. 139) * ■ Transparency 5.3B (TG, p. 140) *
Problem 5.4	1 day	6, 12		■ Transparency 5.4 (TG, p. 141) *
Problem 5.5	1 day	9, 11		■ Transparency 5.5 (TG, p. 142) *
Mathematical Reflections		MR 1–4	■ journal	

* optional materials

© Prentice-Hall, Inc.

Lesson Planner

Investigation 6: Choosing Strategies

Mathematical and Problem-Solving Goals

- To select and apply appropriate strategies to make comparisons
- To review when ratio and difference strategies are useful in solving problems
- To use proportional reasoning to fairly apportion available space so that the group is representative of the larger community

Problems in this Investigation

Problem 6.1: Scaling Up or Down *(pages 65–66)*

Problem 6.2: Using Rules of Thumb *(page 67)*

Problem 6.3: Selecting Delegates *(pages 68–72)*

Resource Options for Planning

	Suggested Pacing	Assignment Guide (ACE questions)	Materials for Students	Resources for Teachers
Investigation 6	3 days total	Exercises are in Student Edition, pp. 73–80	■ graphing calculators	■ Additional Practice, Investigation 6 (TG, p. 180)
Problem 6.1	1 day	1, 10, 11, 14	■ centimeter grid paper * ■ inch grid paper * ■ Labsheet 6.ACE *	■ Transparency 6.1 (TG, p. 143) * ■ Centimeter grid paper BLM (TG, p. 149) ■ Inch grid paper BLM (TG, p. 150) ■ Labsheet 6.ACE BLM (TG, p. 120)*
Problem 6.2	1 day	2, 3, 5–8		■ Transparency 6.2 (TG, p. 144) *
Problem 6.3	1 day	4, 9, 12, 13	■ Labsheets 6.3A and 6.3B (1 of each per group) * ■ large sheets of paper *	■ Transparency 6.3A (TG, p. 145) * ■ Transparency 6.3B (TG, p. 146) * ■ transparencies of Labsheets 6.3A and 6.3B * ■ Labsheets 6.3A and 6.3B BLM (TG, pp. 118–119)
Mathematical Reflections		MR 1–5	■ journal	

* optional materials

© Prentice-Hall, Inc.

Unit Organizer

Accentuate the Negative

Pacing Options

Investigations and Assessments	Class Time (days)
1 Extending the Number Line (SE, pp. 5–17)	3
2 Adding Integers (SE, pp. 18–33)	3
Check-Up 1 (TG, pp. 84–85)	1/2
3 Subtracting Integers (SE, pp. 34–52)	5
Check-Up 2 (TG, p. 86)	1/2
4 Multiplying and Dividing Integers (SE, pp. 53–66)	5
5 Coordinate Grids (SE, pp. 67–82)	5
Looking Back and Looking Ahead: Unit Reflections (SE, pp. 83–85)	1
Self-Assessment (TG, p. 94)	take home
Unit Test (TG, pp. 90–92)	1

Teacher's Guide and Ancillary Resources

Assessment Resources (pp. 83–100)

Blackline Masters (pp. 101–139)

Additional Practice (pp. 141–150)

 Assessment and Additional Practice

Essential Vocabulary

absolute value	number sequence
integer	opposites
negative integer, negative number	positive integer, positive number

Prerequisite Units

None

NCTM Principles and Standards 2000

Content Standard: Number and Operations

Process Standards: Problem Solving, Reasoning and Proof, Communication, Connections, and Representation

Materials

Graphing calculators

Chips or tiles in two colors (about 15–25 of each color per pair of students)

Chip boards (optional; provided as blackline masters)

Colored pens, markers, or pencils (optional)

Number lines (provided as blackline masters)

Coordinate grids (provided as blackline masters)

Graphing calculator grids (provided as blackline masters)

Paper clips

Transparencies of number lines, chip boards, coordinate grids, and graphing calculator grids (optional; provided as blackline masters)

Transparency of Labsheet 4.3 (optional)

Transparent chips or tiles in two colors

Overhead graphing calculator (optional)

Mathematics in the Unit

- Develop strategies for adding, subtracting, multiplying, and dividing integers.
- Determine whether one integer is greater than, less than, or equal to another integer.
- Represent integers on a number line.
- Model situations with integers.
- Use integers to solve problems.
- Explore the use of integers in real-world applications.
- Compare integers using the symbols $=$, $>$, and $<$.
- Understand that an integer and its inverse are called opposites.
- Graph in four quadrants.
- Set up a coordinate grid on a graphing calculator by naming the scale and maximum and minimum values of x and y.
- Graph linear equations using a graphing calculator.
- Informally observe the effects of opposite coefficients and of adding a constant to $y = ax$.
- Answer questions using equations, tables, and graphs.

© Prentice-Hall, Inc.

Connections to Other Units

The ideas in *Accentuate the Negative* build on and connect to several big ideas in
other Connected Mathematics units.

Big Idea	Prior Work	Future Work
defining and developing understanding of negative integers	developing understanding of whole numbers and rational numbers *(Prime Time; Bits and Pieces II)*	interpreting and applying positive and negative slopes of lines and positive and negative coefficients in equations *(Moving Straight Ahead; Thinking with Mathematical Models; Say It with Symbols)*
exploring relationships between positive and negative integers (e.g., interpreting positive integers as a gain and negative integers as a loss)	using models to develop understanding of mathematical concepts *(Covering and Surrounding; Ruins of Montarek; Stretching and Shrinking)*	understanding relationships between positive and negative coefficients in equations *(Thinking with Mathematical Models; Say It with Symbols)*; using positive and negative integers to communicate directions in two dimensions *(Kaleidoscopes, Hubcaps, and Mirrors)*
developing understanding of arithmetic operations with positive and negative integers	understanding and applying arithmetic operations with rational numbers *(Bits and Pieces II; Comparing and Scaling)*	evaluating algebraic expressions involving positive and negative coefficients or values for variables *(Moving Straight Ahead; Thinking with Mathematical Models; Frogs, Fleas, and Painted Cubes; Say It with Symbols; Clever Counting)*; interpreting isometries in the plane given in symbolic form *(Kaleidoscopes, Hubcaps, and Mirrors)*
extending the coordinate grid to include negative coordinates	using a coordinate grid with positive coordinates *(Data About Us; Covering and Surrounding; Variables and Patterns; Stretching and Shrinking)*	graphing equations on coordinate grids *(Moving Straight Ahead; Thinking with Mathematical Models; Growing, Growing, Growing; Frogs, Fleas, and Painted Cubes; Say It with Symbols; Kaleidoscopes, Hubcaps, and Mirrors)*

© Prentice-Hall, Inc.

Lesson Planner

Investigation 1: Extending the Number Line

Mathematical and Problem-Solving Goals

■ To explore the use of integers in applied settings

■ To compare integers using the symbols =, >, and <

■ To represent integers on a number line

■ To understand that an integer and its inverse are called opposites

Problems in this Investigation

Problem 1.1: Playing MathMania *(pages 6–7)*

Problem 1.2: Winning the Game *(pages 8–9)*

Problem 1.3: Measuring Temperature *(pages 9–11)*

Resource Options for Planning

	Suggested Pacing	Assignment Guide (ACE questions)	Materials for Students	Resources for Teachers
Investigation 1	3 days total	Exercises are in Student Edition, pp. 12–16		■ Additional Practice, Investigation 1 (TG, pp. 142–143)
Problem 1.1	1 day	1–7, 27		■ Transparency 1.1A (TG, p. 104) * ■ Transparency 1.1B (TG, p. 105) *
Problem 1.2	1 day	9–14, 26		■ Transparency 1.2 (TG, p. 106) *
Problem 1.3	1 day	8, 15–25, 28, 29		■ Transparency 1.3 (TG, p. 107) *
Mathematical Reflections		MR 1–3	■ journal	

* optional materials

© Prentice-Hall, Inc.

Investigation 2: Adding Integers

Mathematical and Problem-Solving Goals

- To explore addition of integers using two models (a number line and a chip board)
- To develop strategies for adding integers
- To recognize and solve problems involving addition of integers

Problems in this Investigation

Problem 2.1: Adding on a Number Line *(pages 19–21)*

Problem 2.2: Inventing a New Model *(pages 21–25)*

Resource Options for Planning

	Suggested Pacing	Assignment Guide (ACE questions)	Materials for Students	Resources for Teachers
Investigation 2	3 days total	Exercises are in Student Edition, pp. 26–32	■ graphing calculators	■ Additional Practice, Investigation 2 (TG, pp. 144–145)
Problem 2.1	1 day	1–7, 29	■ number lines	■ Transparency 2.1A (TG, p. 108) * ■ transparency of number line * ■ Number line BLM (TG, p. 133)
Problem 2.2 **Mathematical Reflections**	2 days MR 1–3	8–28, 30–37	■ chip boards * ■ chips or tiles in two colors (about 15–25 of each color per pair of students) ■ journal	■ Transparency 2.2 (TG, p. 109) * ■ transparency of chip boards * ■ Chip board BLM (TG, pp. 134–135) ■ transparent chips or tiles in two colors *

* optional materials

© Prentice-Hall, Inc.

Lesson Planner

Investigation 3: Subtracting Integers

Mathematical and Problem-Solving Goals

- To explore subtraction of integers using two models (a number line and a chip board)
- To develop strategies for subtracting integers
- To recognize and use the relationship of addition and subtraction as inverse operations
- To recognize and solve problems involving subtraction of integers

Problems in this Investigation

Problem 3.1: Subtracting on a Chip Board *(pages 35–39)*

Problem 3.2: Subtracting on a Number Line *(pages 40–42)*

Problem 3.3: Exploring Patterns *(page 43)*

Problem 3.4: "Undoing" with Addition and Subtraction *(pages 44–45)*

Resource Options for Planning

	Suggested Pacing	Assignment Guide (ACE questions)	Materials for Students	Resources for Teachers
Investigation 3	5 days total	Exercises are in Student Edition, pp. 46–51	■ graphing calculators	■ Additional Practice, Investigation 3 (TG, pp. 146–147) *
Problem 3.1	1 day	11–14, 34	■ chip boards * ■ chips or tiles in two colors (about 15–25 of each color per pair of students)	■ Transparency 3.1A (TG, p. 110) * ■ Transparency 3.1B (TG, p. 111) * ■ transparency of chip boards * ■ Chip board BLM (TG, pp. 134–135)* ■ transparent chips or tiles in two colors *
Problem 3.2	1 day	1–10, 15–20	■ number lines	■ Transparency 3.2 (TG, p. 112) * ■ transparency of number line * ■ Number line BLM (TG, p. 133)
Problem 3.3	1 day	25–32, 35–38	■ chip boards ■ number lines *	■ Transparency 3.3 (TG, p. 113) * ■ transparency of chip boards * ■ transparency of number line * ■ Chip board BLM (TG, pp. 134–135) ■ Number line BLM (TG, p. 133)
Problem 3.4	2 days	21–24, 33, 39, 40	■ chip boards * ■ chips or tiles in two colors	■ Transparency 3.4 (TG, p. 114) * ■ transparency of chip boards * ■ Chip board BLM (TG, pp. 134–135) ■ transparent chips or tiles in two colors*
Mathematical Reflections		MR 1–5	■ journal	

* optional materials

© Prentice-Hall, Inc.

Investigation 4: Multiplying and Dividing Integers

Mathematical and Problem-Solving Goals

- To develop strategies for multiplying and dividing integers
- To recognize and use the relationship of multiplication and division as inverse operations
- To recognize and solve problems involving multiplication and division of integers

Problems in this Investigation

Problem 4.1: Rising and Falling Temperatures *(pages 53–55)*

Problem 4.2: Studying Multiplication Patterns *(pages 56–57)*

Problem 4.3: Playing the Integer Product Game *(pages 57–58)*

Problem 4.4: Dividing Integers *(page 59)*

Resource Options for Planning

	Suggested Pacing	Assignment Guide (ACE questions)	Materials for Students	Resources for Teachers
Investigation 4	5 days total	Exercises are in Student Edition, pp. 60–65	■ graphing calculator	■ Additional Practice, Investigation 4 (TG, pp. 148–149)
Problem 4.1	1 day	1–3		■ Transparency 4.1A (TG, p. 115) * ■ Transparency 4.1B (TG, p. 116) *
Problem 4.2	1 day	26, 29, 32		■ Transparency 4.2 (TG, p. 117) *
Problem 4.3	1 day	4–8, 17–21, 34	■ Labsheet 4.3 (1 per pair) ■ chips or tiles in two colors (about 12 of each color per pair of students) or colored pens, marker, or pencils ■ paper clips (2 per pair)	■ Transparency 4.3 (TG, p. 118) * ■ transparency of Labsheet 4.3 * ■ Labsheet 4.3 BLM (TG, p. 102) ■ colored transparency markers *
Problem 4.4 **Mathematical Reflections**	2 days	9–16, 22–25, 27, 28, 30, 31, 33, 35–38 MR 1, 2	 ■ journal	■ Transparency 4.4 (TG, p. 119) *

* optional materials

© Prentice-Hall, Inc.

Lesson Planner

Investigation 5: Coordinate Grids

Mathematical and Problem-Solving Goals

- To locate points and lines on a coordinate grid using all four quadrants
- To set up a coordinate grid on a graphing calculator by naming the scale and maximum and minimum values of x and y
- To graph linear equations using a graphing calculator
- To informally observe the effects of opposite coefficients and adding a constant to $y = ax$
- To answer questions using equations, tables, and graphs

Problems in this Investigation

Problem 5.1: Extending the Coordinate Grid *(pages 67–70)*

Problem 5.2: Breaking Even *(pages 71–72)*

Problem 5.3: Using a Calculator to Explore Lines *(pages 72–73)*

Problem 5.4: Exploring Window Settings (pages 73–75)

Problem 5.5: Revisiting Jean's Problem *(pages 75–76)*

Resource Options for Planning

	Suggested Pacing	Assignment Guide (ACE questions)	Materials for Students	Resources for Teachers
Investigation 5	5 days total	Exercises are in Student Edition, pp. 77–81	■ graphing calculators ■ coordinate grids ■ graphing calculator grids	■ Additional Practice, Investigation 5 (TG, p. 150) ■ transparency of coordinate grid * ■ transparency of graphing calculator grid * ■ Coordinate grid BLM (TG, p. 136) ■ Graphing calculator grid BLM (TG, p. 137)
Problem 5.1	1 day	2–5, 13	■ grid paper *	■ Transparency 5.1A (TG, p. 120) * ■ Transparency 5.1B (TG, p. 121) * ■ Transparency 5.1C (TG, p. 122) * ■ Grid paper BLM (TG, p. 139)*
Problem 5.2	1 day	6, 11		■ Transparency 5.2 (TG, p. 123) *
Problem 5.3	1 day	14		■ Transparency 5.3A (TG, p. 124) * ■ Transparency 5.3B (TG, p. 125) *
Problem 5.4	1 day	1, 7–10, 12	■ grid paper ■ Labsheet 5.ACE	■ Transparency 5.4A (TG, p. 126) * ■ Transparency 5.4B (TG, p. 127) * ■ Transparency 5.4C (TG, p. 128) * ■ Transparency 5.4D (TG, p. 129) * ■ Grid paper BLM (TG, p. 139) * ■ Labsheet 5.ACE BLM (TG, p. 103)
Problem 5.5 **Mathematical Reflections**	1 day	Unassigned choices from earlier problems MR 1, 2	■ journal	■ Transparency 5.5 (TG, p. 130) *

* optional materials

© Prentice-Hall, Inc.

Accentuate the Negative

Unit Organizer

Moving Straight Ahead

Pacing Options

Investigations and Assessments	Class Time (days)
1 Predicting from Patterns (SE, pp. 5–14)	2
2 Walking Rates (SE, pp. 15–34)	6
Check-Up (TG, pp. 95–96)	1/2
3 Exploring Lines with a Graphing Calculator (SE, pp. 35–52)	5
Quiz A (TG, pp. 97–99)	1
4 Solving Equations (SE, pp. 53–63)	5
5 Exploring Slope (SE, pp. 64–79	3
Quiz B (TG, pp. 100–101)	1
6 Writing an Equation for a Line (SE, pp. 80–91)	4
Looking Back and Looking Ahead: Unit Reflections (SE, pp. 92–94)	1
Self-Assessment (TG, p. 110)	take home
Unit Test (TG, pp. 105–108)	1

Teacher's Guide and Ancillary Resources

Assessment Resources (pp. 93–125)

Blackline Masters (pp. 127–158)

Additional Practice (pp. 159–168)

 Assessment and Additional Practice

Essential Vocabulary

coefficient

coordinate pair

linear, linear relationship

point of intersection

rise

run

slope

y-intercept

Prerequisite Units

Variables and Patterns (Algebra)

Accentuate the Negative (Number and Operations)

NCTM Principles and Standards 2000

Content Standard: Algebra

Process Standards: Problem Solving, Reasoning and Proof, Communication, Connections, and Representation

Materials

Graphing calculators

Materials for the experiments in Investigation 1: 12-oz waxed paper cups, paper clips, clear graduated cylinders or other measuring containers, clocks or other timers, water, balls (golf balls, tennis balls, table tennis balls) and metersticks

String

Transparent grids (optional)

Overhead graphing calculator

Strips of balsa wood (optional)

Transparencies of the graph, table, and equations from Problem 2.3 (optional)

Set of stairs

Tape measure

Mathematics in the Unit

- Further develop understanding of variables and patterns (continuing the exploration of the ideas presented in the *Variables and Patterns* unit).

- Recognize and represent the relationships among variables in a variety of ways, including the use of words, tables, graphs, and symbols.

- Identify variables and determine an appropriate range of values for independent and dependent variables.

- Collect data and use patterns in tables and graphs to make predictions.

- Use graphing calculators to study linear relationships.

- Communicate with and interpret information from a variety of representations.

- Recognize linear situations in all representations: written descriptions, tables, graphs, and symbols.

- Recognize that linearity is associated with a constant rate of change between two variables.

- Recognize a change in the slope or the *y*-intercept and its effect on the various representations.

- Solve a linear function of the form $y = mx + b$ using tables, graphs, and equations.

- Find the slope and the *y*-intercept of a linear equation and interpret the meaning of each.

- Write a linear equation with the slope and *y*-intercept.

- Find a solution common to two linear equations by graphing or creating tables.

© Prentice-Hall, Inc.

Connections to Other Units

The ideas in *Moving Straight Ahead* build on and connect to several big ideas in other Connected Mathematics units.

Big Idea	Prior Work	Future Work
identifying, representing, and interpreting linear relationships in tabular, graphical, and symbolic forms	graphing data in the coordinate plane; using symbols to represent relationships between variables (*Variables and Patterns; Accentuate the Negative*)	identifying and interpreting equations for linear ($y = mx + b$), exponential ($y = a^x$), quadratic ($y = ax^2 + bx + c$), and nonlinear (e.g., $y = \frac{k}{x}$) relationships (*Thinking with Mathematical Models; Growing, Growing, Growing; Frogs, Fleas, and Painted Cubes; Say It with Symbols*)
writing and interpreting linear equations in $y = mx + b$ form	expressing relationships between variables in words, symbols, graphs, and tables (*Variables and Patterns*)	writing and interpreting equations that express linear, nonlinear, quadratic, and exponential relationships (*Thinking with Mathematical Models; Growing, Growing, Growing; Frogs, Fleas, and Painted Cubes; Say It with Symbols*)
finding and interpreting the point of intersection of two lines	understanding the meaning of parallel and intersecting lines (*Shapes and Designs*)	finding and interpreting points of intersection in graphs and mathematical models (*Thinking with Mathematical Models*); interpreting parallel, intersecting, and perpendicular lines (*Looking for Pythagoras*); analyzing equivalent linear expressions (*Say It with Symbols*)
finding the slope of a line; interpreting slope as the ratio of vertical change to horizontal change	computing and interpreting ratios (*Bits and Pieces I; Bits and Pieces II; Comparing and Scaling*); Finding rates of change in relationships between variables (*Variables and Patterns*); understanding positive and negative numbers (*Accentuate the Negative*)	analyzing linear models; interpreting slope as a rate of change (*Thinking with Mathematical Models*); interpreting slope in linear relationships (*Looking for Pythagoras*); finding the slope of a line to determine an equation in $y = mx + b$ form (*Say It with Symbols*)
identifying x- and y-intercepts from a graph or an equation	graphing relationships between variables (*Variables and Patterns*)	interpreting and constructing graphs of lines; determining the equation of a line (*Thinking with Mathematical Models; Say It with Symbols*)

© Prentice-Hall, Inc.

Investigation 1: Predicting From Patterns

Mathematical and Problem-Solving Goals

- To encounter the idea that many phenomena are constrained by linear relationships
- To collect data and use patterns in tables and graphs to make predictions
- To connect points of a graph of data that were collected or predicted

Problems in this Investigation

Problem 1.1: Conducting an Experiment *(pages 5–8)*

Resource Options for Planning

	Suggested Pacing	Assignment Guide (ACE questions)	Materials for Students	Resources for Teachers
Investigation 1	2 days total	Exercises are in Student Edition, pp. 9–13	■ graphing calculators ■ centimeter or half-centimeter grid paper ■ blank transparencies	■ Additional Practice, Investigation 1 (TG, p. 172) ■ Centimeter or half-centimeter grid BLM (TG, p. 157 or 158)
Problem 1.1A	1 day	1–9	■ 12-oz waxed paper cups ■ paper clips ■ clear graduated cylinders or other measuring containers ■ clocks or other timers ■ water	■ Transparency 1.1A (TG, p. 128) * ■ Transparency 1.1C (TG, p. 130) *
Problem 1.1B	1 day		■ balls (golf balls, tennis balls, table tennis balls) ■ metersticks	■ Transparency 1.1B (TG, p. 129) * ■ Transparency 1.1D (TG, p. 131) *
Mathematical Reflections		MR 1, 2	■ journal	

* optional materials

© Prentice-Hall, Inc.

Investigation 2: Walking Rates

Mathematical and Problem-Solving Goals

■ To recognize linear relationships from tables: for each unit change in one variable, there is a constant rate of change in the other variable

■ To determine whether a set of data is linear by examining its graph

■ To recognize how the rate of change between two variables is associated with its representations

■ To recognize that a change in rate will change the steepness of a line and the coefficient of x (the independent variable)

■ To interpret the meaning of the coefficient of x and the y-intercept of a graph of $y = mx + b$

Problems in this Investigation

Problem 2.1: Walking to the Yogurt Shop *(page 17)*

Problem 2.2: Changing the Walking Rate *(pages 18–19)*

Problem 2.3: Walking for Charity *(pages 19–20)*

Problem 2.4: Walking to Win *(page 21)*

Problem 2.5: Crossing the Line *(pages 22–23)*

Resource Options for Planning

	Suggested Pacing	Assignment Guide (ACE questions)	Materials for Students	Resources for Teachers
Investigation 2	6 days total	Exercises are in Student Edition, pp. 24–33	■ graphing calculators ■ grid paper	■ Additional Practice, Investigation 2 (TG, p. 173) ■ transparent grids ■ Centimeter grid paper BLM (TG, p. 158) ■ overhead graphing calculator *
Problem 2.1	1 day	14–17		■ Transparency 2.1 (TG, p. 132) *
Problem 2.2	1 day	1–5, 7–9		■ Transparency 2.2 (TG, p. 133) *
Problem 2.3	1 day	6, 18–20		■ Transparency 2.3A (TG, p. 134) * ■ Transparency 2.3B (TG, p. 135) *
Problem 2.4	1 day	10–12		■ Transparency 2.4 (TG, p. 136) *
Problem 2.5 **Mathematical Reflections**	2 days	13, 21, 22 MR 1–4	■ blank transparencies or large sheets of paper * ■ journal	■ Transparency 2.5 (TG, p. 137) *

* optional materials

© Prentice-Hall, Inc.

Lesson Planner

Investigation 3: Exploring Lines with a Graphing Calculator

Mathematical and Problem-Solving Goals

- To connect solutions in graphs and tables to solutions of equations
- To find a solution common to two linear equations by graphing
- To understand how the *y*-intercept appears in tables and equations
- To understand how the rate of change (the coeffiecient *m*) appears in equations and affects the graph of a line

Problems in this Investigation

Problem 3.1: Getting to the Point *(page 36)*

Problem 3.2: Graphing Lines *(pages 37–39)*

Problem 3.3: Finding Solutions *(pages 39–40)*

Problem 3.4: Planning a Skating Party *(pages 41–43)*

Resource Options for Planning

	Suggested Pacing	Assignment Guide (ACE questions)	Materials for Students	Resources for Teachers
Investigation 3	5 days total	Exercises are in Student Edition, pp. 44–51	■ graphing calculators	■ Additional Practice, Investigation 3 (TG, pp. 174–175) ■ overhead graphing calculator *
Problem 3.1	1 day	24–26		■ Transparency 3.1A (TG, p. 138) * ■ transparencies of the graph, table, and equations from Problem 2.3 *
Problem 3.2	1 day	1–4, 6, 27		■ Transparency 3.2A (TG, p. 139) * ■ Transparency 3.2B (TG, p. 140) *
Problem 3.3	1 day	18–21, 28, 29		■ Transparency 3.3A (TG, p. 141) * ■ Transparency 3.3B (TG, p. 142) *
Problem 3.4	2 days	5–17, 22, 23		■ Transparency 3.ACE (TG, p. 143) *
Mathematical Reflections		MR 1–4	■ journal	

* optional materials

© Prentice-Hall, Inc.

Investigation 4: Solving Equations

Mathematical and Problem-Solving Goals

- To solve an equation of the form $y = mx + b$ symbolically
- To connect various methods of finding information in graphs and in tables and by solving equations

Problems in this Investigation

Problem 4.1: Paying in Installments *(page 53)*

Problem 4.2: Using the Symbolic Method *(pages 54–56)*

Problem 4.3: Analyzing Bones *(pages 57–58)*

Resource Options for Planning

	Suggested Pacing	Assignment Guide (ACE questions)	Materials for Students	Resources for Teachers
Investigation 1	5 days total	Exercises are in Student Edition, pp. 59–62	■ graphing calculators	■ Additional Practice, Investigation 4 (TG, pp. 176–177) ■ overhead graphing calculator * ■ transparent grids *
Problem 4.1	2 days	1–3, 11, 13, 16		■ Transparency 4.1 (TG, p. 144) *
Problem 4.2	1 day	4–8, 12		■ Transparency 4.2A (TG, p. 145) * ■ Transparency 4.2B (TG, p. 146) * ■ Transparency 4.2C (TG, p. 147) *
Problem 4.3	2 days	9, 10, 14, 15, 17	■ blank transparencies or large sheets of paper * ■ rulers or tape measures ■ journal	■ Transparency 4.3 (TG, p. 148) *
Mathematical Reflections		MR 1, 2		

* optional materials

© Prentice-Hall, Inc.

Investigation 5: Exploring Slope

Mathematical and Problem-Solving Goals

- To develop a more formal understanding of the concept of slope
- To find the constant rate, or slope, from a table
- To find the slope of a line given two points on the line
- To relate the slope and the *y*-intercept to the equation of a line

Problems in this Investigation

Problem 5.1: Climbing Stairs *(pages 64–66)*

Problem 5.2: Finding the Slope of a Line *(pages 66–68)*

Problem 5.3: Connecting Points *(pages 68–69)*

Resource Options for Planning

	Suggested Pacing	Assignment Guide (ACE questions)	Materials for Students	Resources for Teachers
Investigation 5	3 days total	Exercises are in Student Edition, pp. 70–78	■ graphing calculators ■ grid paper	■ Additional Practice, Investigation 5 (TG, pp. 178–179) ■ transparent grids * ■ overhead graphing calculator *
Problem 5.1	1 day	1–4, 26, 28, 29	■ set of stairs to measure ■ tape measures ■ string	■ Transparency 5.1 (TG, p. 149) *
Problem 5.2	1 day	5–9, 18–20, 24, 25, 32, 33		■ Transparency 5.2 (TG, p. 150) *
Problem 5.3 **Mathematical Reflections**	1 day	10–17, 21–23, 27, 30, 31 MR 1–4	■ blank transparencies * ■ journal	■ Transparency 5.3 (TG, p. 151) *

* optional materials

© Prentice-Hall, Inc.

Investigation 6: Writing an Equation for a Line

Mathematical and Problem-Solving Goals

- To find the equation of a line given two points
- To review important ideas about linear relationships
- To use knowledge about linear relationships to solve problems

Problems in this Investigation

Problem 6.1: Solving Alphonso's Puzzle *(page 80)*

Problem 6.2: Converting Temperatues *(page 81)*

Problem 6.3: Solving the Mystery of the Irish Elk *(pages 82–83)*

Resource Options for Planning

	Suggested Pacing	Assignment Guide (ACE questions)	Materials for Students	Resources for Teachers
Investigation 6	4 days total	Exercises are in Student Edition, pp. 84–90	■ graphing calculators ■ grid paper *	■ Additional Practice, Investigation 6 (TG, p. 180) ■ overhead graphing calculator * ■ transparent grids *
Problem 6.1	1 day	1–13		■ Transparency 6.1 (TG, p. 152) *
Problem 6.2	1 day	14–20, 26		■ Transparency 6.2 (TG, p. 153) *
Problem 6.3	2 days	21–25, 27–30	■ grid paper *	■ Transparency 6.3 (TG, p. 154) * ■ strips of balsa wood *
Mathematical Reflections		MR 1–3	■ journal	.

* optional materials

© Prentice-Hall, Inc.

Unit Organizer

Filling and Wrapping

Pacing Options

Investigations and Assessments	Class Time (days)
1 Building Boxes (SE, pp. 5–14)	4
2 Designing Packages (SE, pp. 15–23)	2
3 Finding Volumes of Boxes (SE, pp. 24–36)	3
Check-Up 1 (TG, p. 77)	1/2
4 Cylinders (SE, pp. 37–45)	4
5 Cones and Spheres (SE, pp. 46–56)	3
Check-Up 2 (TG, pp. 78–79)	1/2
6 Scaling Boxes (SE, pp. 57–67)	3
Quiz (TG, pp. 80–82)	1
7 Finding Volumes of Irregular Objects (SE, pp. 68–72)	1
Looking Back and Looking Ahead: Unit Reflections (SE, pp. 74–76)	1
Self-Assessment (TG, p. 89)	take home
Unit Test (TG, pp. 85–86)	1
Unit Project (SE, p. 73, optional)	take home

Teacher's Guide and Ancillary Resources

Assessment Resources (pp. 75–106)

Blackline Masters (pp. 107–137)

Additional Practice (pp. 139–149)

 Assessment and Additional Practice

Essential Vocabulary

base	prism
cone	rectangular prism
cube	sphere
cylinder	surface area
edge	unit cube
face	volume
flat pattern	

Prerequisite Units

Shapes and Designs (Geometry, Measurement)

Stretching and Shrinking (Geometry, Measurement)

Comparing and Scaling (Number and Operations, Algebra)

NCTM Principles and Standards 2000

Content Standard: Geometry, Measurement

Process Standards: Problem Solving, Reasoning and Proof, Communication, Connections, and Representation

Materials

Centimeter cubes and inch cubes

Small cardboard boxes and cylindrical cans

Modeling dough

Sand or rice (about a half cup per group)

Clear plastic containers marked in milliliters

Stones and other irregularly shaped objects

Assorted prisms, spheres, cones, and cylinders, including some with the same height and radius

Assorted flat patterns (some with flaps) that can be folded into boxes (many stores have gift boxes that come flat)

News clippings of local waste-disposal issues (optional)

Mathematics in the Unit

■ Conceptualize volume as a measure of *filling* an object.

■ Develop the concept of volumes for prisms and cylinders as stacking layers of unit cubes to fill the object.

■ Conceptualize surface area as a measure of *wrapping* an object.

■ Discover that strategies for finding the volume and the surface area of a rectangular prism will work for any prism.

■ Explore the relationship of the surface areas of rectangular prisms and cylinders to the total area of a flat pattern needed to wrap the solid.

■ Discover the relationships among the volumes of cylinders, cones, and spheres.

■ Reason about problems involving the surface areas and volumes of rectangular prisms, cylinders, cones, and spheres.

■ Investigate the effects of varying dimensions of rectangular prisms and cylinders on volume and surface area and vice versa.

■ Estimate the volume of an irregular shape by measuring the amount of water displaced by the solid.

■ Understand the relationship between a cubic centimeter and a milliliter.

© Prentice-Hall, Inc.

Connections to Other Units

The ideas in *Filling and Wrapping* build on and connect to several big ideas in other Connected Mathematics units.

Big Idea	Prior Work	Future Work
understanding, calculating, and estimating the surface area of 3-D figures	understanding, calculating, and estimating the perimeter of 2-D figures *(Covering and Surrounding)*	using surface area of cubes to build understanding of quadratic growth *(Frogs, Fleas, and Painted Cubes)*
understanding, calculating, and estimating the volume of 3-D figures	understanding, calculating, and estimating the area of 2-D figures *(Covering and Surrounding)*	using equations of nonlinear relationships *(Say It with Symbols)*
finding and interpreting the dimensions, surface area, and volume of rectangular prisms	understanding what the dimensions of a figure are *(Shapes and Designs)*; finding and interpreting perimeter and area of 2-D figures *(Covering and Surrounding)*; studying the structure of 3-D cubic figures *(Ruins of Montarek)*	studying maximum and minimum values and mathematical models *(Thinking with Mathematical Models)*; developing counting strategies *(Clever Counting)*
developing strategies for finding the dimensions, surface area, and volume of cylinders, cones, and spheres	studying relationships between triangles, rectangles, and parallelograms; developing strategies for finding the perimeter and area of 2-D figures with straight edges *(Shapes and Designs; Covering and Surrounding)*	studying quadratic ($y = ax^2 + bx + c$) and exponential ($y = kx^a$) relationships *(Thinking with Mathematical Models; Growing, Growing, Growing; Frogs, Fleas, and Painted Cubes)*
scaling 3-D figures	enlarging, shrinking, and distorting 2-D figures *(Stretching and Shrinking)*; scaling quantities up and down using ratios and proportions *(Comparing and Scaling)*	studying exponential growth (e.g., $y = kx^2$ and $y = kx^3$) *(Growing, Growing, Growing; Frogs, Fleas, and Painted Cubes; Data Around Us)*
developing strategies for estimating the surface area and volume of irregular 3-D figures	developing strategies for estimating the perimeter and area of irregular 2-D figures *(Covering and Surrounding)*	developing strategies for making inferences about samples and populations *(Samples and Populations; Data Around Us)*

© Prentice-Hall, Inc.

Lesson Planner

Investigation 1: Building Boxes

Mathematical and Problem-Solving Goals

- To develop the concept of surface area by counting the number of unit squares needed to wrap (enclose) a rectangular box

- To explore the relationship between the surface area of a box and the total area of the unit squares needed to wrap the box

- To develop the concept of volume of a rectangular box, and strategies for finding it, by filling a box with unit cubes

Problems in this Investigation

Problem 1.1: Making Cubic Boxes *(pages 5–6)*

Problem 1.2: Making Rectangular Boxes *(page 7)*

Problem 1.3: Flattening a Box *(page 8)*

Problem 1.4: Testing Flat Patterns *(page 9)*

Resource Options for Planning

	Suggested Pacing	Assignment Guide (ACE questions)	Materials for Students	Resources for Teachers
Investigation 1	4 days total	Exercises are in Student Edition, pp. 10–13	■ graphing calculators ■ inch and centimeter grid paper ■ metric rulers ■ scissors ■ transparent tape ■ glue	■ Additional Practice, Investigation 1 (TG, pp. 140–141) ■ Centimeter grid paper BLM (TG, p. 134) ■ Inch grid paper BLM (TG, p. 136)
Problem 1.1	1 day	1a, 2–5, 9, 11–16		■ Transparency 1.1A (TG, p. 111) * ■ Transparency 1.1B (TG, p. 112) *
Problem 1.2	1 day	1b, 8		■ Transparency 1.2A (TG, p. 113) * ■ Transparency 1.2B (TG, p. 114) *
Problem 1.3	1 day	10, 19	■ small cardboard boxes (1 per pair)	■ Transparency 1.3 (TG, p. 115) * ■ assorted rectangular boxes ■ assorted flat patterns
Problem 1.4	1 day	6, 7, 17, 18	■ Labsheet 1.4 (1 per pair) ■ centimeter cubes (15–20 per pair) ■ inch cubes (1 per student) ■ Labsheet 1.ACE (1 per student) *	■ Transparency 1.4 (TG, p. 116) * ■ transparency of Labsheet 1.4 * ■ Labsheet 1.4 BLM (TG, p. 108) ■ Labsheet 1.ACE BLM (TG, p. 109) *
Mathematical Reflections		MR 1–4	■ journal	

* optional materials

© Prentice-Hall, Inc.

Investigation 2: Designing Packages

Mathematical and Problem-Solving Goals

- To develop strategies for finding the surface area of a rectangular box
- To determine which rectangular prism has the least (greatest) surface area for a fixed volume
- To reason about problems involving surface area

Problems in this Investigation

Problem 2.1: Packaging Blocks *(page 16)*

Problem 2.2: Saving Trees *(pages 17–18)*

Resource Options for Planning

	Suggested Pacing	Assignment Guide (ACE questions)	Materials for Students	Resources for Teachers
Investigation 2	2 days total	Exercises are in Student Edition, pp. 19–22	■ graphing calculators ■ centimeter cubes (about 30 per student)	■ Additional Practice, Investigation 2 (TG, pp. 142–143)
Problem 2.1	1 day	1–7, 10		■ Transparency 2.1 (TG, p. 117) *
Problem 2.2	1 day	8, 9, 11–13		■ Transparency 2.2 (TG, p. 118) *
Mathematical Reflections		MR 1–2	■ journal	

* optional materials

© Prentice-Hall, Inc.

Lesson Planner

Investigation 3: Finding Volumes of Boxes

Mathematical and Problem-Solving Goals

- To develop a strategy for finding the volume of a rectangular prism by filling it with unit cubes, and to recognize that the number of cubes in the bottom layer is equal to the area of the base

- To determine that the total number of unit cubes in a rectangular prism is equal to the area of the base times the height (the volume), and to discover that this strategy works for any prism

- To learn that the surface area of a prism is the sum of the areas of its faces, and to apply this strategy to any right prism

- To reason about problems involving volume and surface area

Problems in this Investigation

Problem 3.1: Filling Rectangular Boxes *(pages 24–25)*

Problem 3.2: Burying Garbage *(page 26)*

Problem 3.2: Filling Fancy Boxes *(pages 26–28)*

Resource Options for Planning

	Suggested Pacing	Assignment Guide (ACE questions)	Materials for Students	Resources for Teachers
Investigation 3	3 days total	Exercises are in Student Edition, pp. 29–35	■ graphing calculators	■ Additional Practice, Investigation 3 (TG, p. 144)
Problem 3.1	1 day	1–8. 13	■ centimeter cubes * ■ small cardboard boxes (1 per pair) ■ isometric dot paper	■ Transparency 3.1 (TG, p. 119) * ■ transparent grids * ■ Isometric dot paper BLM (TG, p. 137) ■ Inch grid paper BLM (TG, p. 136)
Problem 3.2	1 day	9, 14–16		■ Transparency 3.2 (TG, p. 120) * ■ news clippings of local waste-disposal issues *
Problem 3.3	1 day	10–12, 17, 18	■ centimeter grid paper (several sheets per group) ■ transparent tape ■ metric rulers ■ plain paper	■ Transparency 3.3 (TG, p. 121) * ■ examples of triangular, rectangular, pentagonal, and hexagonal prisms * ■ small items for filling prisms ■ Centimeter grid paper BLM (TG, p. 134)
Mathematical Reflections		MR 1, 2	■ journal	

* optional materials

© Prentice-Hall, Inc.

Lesson Planner

Investigation 4: Cylinders

Mathematical and Problem-Solving Goals

- To develop strategies for finding the volume and surface area of a cylinder
- To compare the process of finding the volumes and surface areas of cylinders and rectangular prisms
- To investigate interesting problems involving the volumes and surface areas of cylinders and prisms

Problems in this Investigation

Problem 4.1: Filling a Cylinder *(page 38)*

Problem 4.2: Making a Cylinder from a Flat Pattern *(page 39)*

Problem 4.3: Designing a New Juice Container *(page 40)*

Resource Options for Planning

	Suggested Pacing	Assignment Guide (ACE questions)	Materials for Students	Resources for Teachers
Investigation 4	4 days total	Exercises are in Student Edition, pp. 41–44	■ graphing calculators ■ centimeter grid paper (several sheets per student)	■ Additional Practice, ■ Investigation 4 (TG, p. 145) ■ Centimeter grid paper (BLM, TG, p. 134)
Problem 4.1	1 day	10, 11	■ plain paper ■ scissors ■ transparent tape ■ metric rulers ■ centimeter cubes	■ Transparency 4.1 (TG, p. 122) * ■ transparent centimeter grid * ■ cylinders and a rectangular prism ■ small items for filling cylinders
Problem 4.2	1 day	1–4, 6	■ Labsheet 4.2 (1 per student) ■ small cylindrical cans ■ centimeter cubes	■ Transparency 4.2 (TG, p. 123) * ■ transparency of Labsheet 4.2 * ■ Labsheet 4.2 BLM (TG, p. 110) ■ cylindrical tennis ball container ■ string
Problem 4.3	2 days	5, 7–9, 12, 13		■ Transparency 4.3 (TG, p. 124) * ■ juice box or can
Mathematical Reflections		MR 1–4	■ journal	

* optional materials

© Prentice-Hall, Inc.

Investigation 5: Cones and Spheres

Mathematical and Problem-Solving Goals

- To develop strategies for finding the volumes of cones and spheres
- To find the relationships among the volumes of cylinders, cones, and spheres
- To reason about problems involving cylinders, cones, and spheres

Problems in this Investigation

Problem 5.1: Comparing Spheres and Cylinders *(pages 47–48)*
Problem 5.2: Comparing Cones and Cylinders *(pages 49–50)*
Problem 5.3: Melting Ice Cream *(page 50)*

Resource Options for Planning

	Suggested Pacing	Assignment Guide (ACE questions)	Materials for Students	Resources for Teachers
Investigation 5	3 days total	Exercises are in Student Edition, pp. 51–55	■ graphing calculators	■ Additional Practice, Investigation 5 (TG, pp. 146–147) ■ assorted spheres, cones, and cylinders *
Problem 5.1	1 day	Unassigned choices from earlier problems	■ modeling dough ■ 6-cm to 9-cm strips of transparency film (1 strip per group) ■ transparent tape ■ metric ruler	■ Transparency 5.1 (TG, p. 125) * ■ cylindrical tennis ball container with 3 balls *
Problem 5.2	1 day	1–4, 8, 12	■ sand or rice (about 1/2 cup per group) ■ plain paper ■ transparent tape ■ scissors	■ Transparency 5.2 (TG, p. 126) *
Problem 5.3	1 day	5–7, 9–11		■ Transparency 5.3 (TG, p. 127) *
Mathematical Reflections		MR 1–3	■ journal	

* optional materials

© Prentice-Hall, Inc.

Lesson Planner

Investigation 6: Scaling Boxes

Mathematical and Problem-Solving Goals

- To apply strategies for finding the volumes of rectangular prisms to designing boxes with given specifications

- To investigate the effects of varying the dimensions of rectangular prisms on volume and surface area and vice versa

Problems in this Investigation

Problem 6.1: Building a Bigger Box *(pages 58–59)*

Problem 6.2: Scaling Up the Compost Box *(page 59)*

Problem 6.3: Looking at Similar Prisms *(page 60)*

Resource Options for Planning

	Suggested Pacing	Assignment Guide (ACE questions)	Materials for Students	Resources for Teachers
Investigation 6	3 days total	Exercises are in Student Edition, pp. 61–66	■ graphing calculators	■ Additional Practice, Investigation 6 (TG, p. 148) ■ demonstration compost boxes
Problem 6.1	1 day	6, 9, 10	■ centimeter cubes * ■ centimeter grid paper ■ scissors ■ transparent tape ■ isometric dot paper *	■ Transparency 6.1 (TG, p. 128) * ■ Centimeter grid paper BLM (TG, p. 134) ■ Isometric dot paper BLM (TG, p. 137) *
Problem 6.2	1 day	1, 3–5, 7, 11	■ centimeter cubes * ■ centimeter grid paper ■ scissors ■ transparent tape ■ isometric dot paper *	■ Transparency 6.2 (TG, p. 129) * ■ Centimeter grid paper BLM (TG, p. 134) ■ Isometric dot paper BLM (TG, p. 137) *
Problem 6.3	1 day	2, 8, 12–22		■ Transparency 6.3 (TG, p. 130) *
Mathematical Reflections		MR 1, 2	■ journal	

* optional materials

© Prentice-Hall, Inc.

Investigation 7: Finding Volumes of Irregular Objects

Mathematical and Problem-Solving Goals

■ To estimate the volume of an irregularly shaped object by measuring the amount of water it displaces

■ To understand the relationship between a cubic centimeter and a milliliter

Problems in this Investigation

Problem 7.1: Displacing Water *(pages 68–69)*

Resource Options for Planning

	Suggested Pacing	Assignment Guide (ACE questions)	Materials for Students	Resources for Teachers
Investigation 7	1 day total	Exercises are in Student Edition, pp. 70–71	■ graphing calculators	■ Additional Practice, Investigation 7 (TG, p. 149)
Problem 7.1	1 day	1–7	■ clear plastic containers marked in milliliters (such as graduated cylinders; 1 per group) ■ metric rulers ■ centimeter cubes (5–10 per group) ■ stones and other irregularly shaped objects ■ clay spheres from Investigation 5 * ■ water	■ Transparency 7.1 (TG, p. 131) * ■ transparent 2-quart measuring container and a stick of butter *
Mathematical Reflections		MR 1, 2	■ journal	

* optional materials

© Prentice-Hall, Inc.

What Do You Expect?

Pacing Options

Investigations and Assessments	Class Time (days)
1 Evaluating Games of Chance (SE, pp. 5–21)	4
2 Analyzing Number-Cube Games (SE, pp. 22–31)	2
Check-Up 1 (TG, pp. 83–84)	1/2
3 Probability and Area (SE, pp. 32–40)	2
Quiz A (TG, pp. 85–86)	1
4 Analyzing Two-Stage Games (SE, pp. 41–49)	3
5 Expected Value (SE, pp. 50–58)	3
Check-Up 2 (TG, p. 87)	1/2
6 Carnival Games (SE, pp. 59–68)	3
Quiz B (TG, p. 88)	1
7 Analyzing Sequences of Outcomes (SE, pp. 69–78)	3
Looking Back and Looking Ahead: Unit Reflections (SE, pp. 81–83)	1
Self-Assessment (TG, p. 98)	take home
Unit Test (TG, pp. 93–94)	1
Unit Project (SE, pp. 79–80)	take home

Teacher's Guide and Ancillary Resources

Assessment Resources (pp. 81–121)

Blackline Masters (pp. 123–162)

Additional Practice (pp. 163–171)

 Assessment and Additional Practice

Essential Vocabulary

counting tree

expected value, long-term average

Prerequisite Units

Prime Time (Number and Operations)

Data About Us (Data Analysis and Probability)

How Likely Is It? (Data Analysis and Probability)

NCTM Principles and Standards 2000

Content Standard: Data Analysis and Probability

Process Standards: Problem Solving, Reasoning and Proof, Communication, Connections, and Representation

Materials

Number cubes (2 per pair)

Colored blocks or other manipulatives

Opaque containers large enough for a student's hand

Computers and the Treasure Hunt program (optional)

10-section, 12-section, and 16-section spinners (optional; provided as BLM)

10 by 10 grids (optional; provided as BLM)

Paper clips or bobby pins (1 per pair)

Coins (1 per group)

Mathematics in the Unit

- More deeply understand experimental and theoretical probabilities and the relationship between them.
- Further develop an understanding of the possible outcomes in a situation.
- More deeply understand the distinction between equally likely and unequally likely outcomes.
- Understand the distinction between single, specific outcomes and sets of outcomes that comprise an event.
- Analyze situations involving either independent or dependent events.
- Understand how to use probabilities and equivalent fractions to find expected value.
- Determine whether games of chance are fair or unfair and find ways to make unfair games fair.
- Develop a variety of strategies for analyzing probabilities, such as using lists, counting trees, and area models.
- Use counting trees for finding theoretical probabilities in binomial, or 50–50, probability situations.
- Determine the expected value of a chance situation.
- Use probability and expected value to make decisions.
- Find probabilities in situations that involve drawing with and without replacement.

© Prentice-Hall, Inc.

Connections to Other Units

The ideas in *What Do You Expect?* build on and connect to several big ideas in other
Connected Mathematics units.

Big Idea	Prior Work	Future Work
understanding probability	understanding chance as the likelihood of a particular event occurring; studying equally likely outcomes and randomness (*How Likely Is It?*); interpreting decimals, fractions, and percents as probabilities (*Bits and Pieces II*)	using probabilities to make inferences and predictions about populations based on analysis of population samples (*Samples and Populations*)
understanding, determining, and reasoning with experimental probability	conducting trials of a game or experiment to determine experimental probabilities (*How Likely Is It?*); organizing data collected from experiments (*Variables and Patterns; Moving Straight Ahead*)	using data collected from samples of populations to determine experimental probabilities; developing techniques for simulating situations in order to collect and organize data (*Samples and Populations*)
understanding, determining, and reasoning with theoretical probability	analyzing simple games to determine theoretical probabilities (*How Likely Is It?*); interpreting fractions, decimals, and percents as a ratio of the number of desired outcomes to the number of all possible outcomes (*Bits and Pieces II*)	developing strategies for analyzing complex games or situations to determine theoretical probabilities (*Samples and Populations*); developing counting strategies to calculate theoretical probabilities (*Clever Counting*)
finding and reasoning with expected value	studying favorable outcomes, equally likely outcomes, and random outcomes (*How Likely Is It?*)	using expected values of favorable and unfavorable outcomes to make inferences and predictions; using expected values to make recommendations or to develop solutions to real-world problems (*Samples and Populations; Clever Counting*)

© Prentice-Hall, Inc.

Lesson Planner

Investigation 1: Evaluating Games of Chance

Mathematical and Problem-Solving Goals

- To review and develop a deeper understanding of experimental and theoretical probabilities and the relationship between them

- To review and extend methods of finding experimental probabilities

- To review and extend methods of finding theoretical probabilities, including making an organized list, or counting tree, of all possible outcomes

- To review the distinction between equally likely and unequally likely outcomes

- To determine whether a game is fair or unfair

- To make unfair games fair by informally applying the concept of expected value

Problems in this Investigation

Problem 1.1: What's in the Bucket? *(pages 5–6)*
Problem 1.2: Matching Colors *(pages 6–7)*
Problem 1.3: Making Purple *(pages 8–9)*
Problem 1.4: Making Counting Trees *(pages 10–12)*

Resource Options for Planning

	Suggested Pacing	Assignment Guide (ACE questions)	Materials for Students	Resources for Teachers
Investigation 1	4 days total	Exercises are in Student Edition, pp. 13–20	■ graphing calculators	■ Additional Practice, Investigation 1 (TG, p. 164)
Problem 1.1	1 day	18		■ Transparency 1.1 (TG, p. 131) * ■ opaque container filled with 4 blue, 8 yellow, and 12 red blocks ■ 16 additional blue blocks
Problem 1.2	1 day	1–7	■ Labsheet 1.2 (1 per pair) ■ paper clips or bobby pins (1 per pair)	■ Transparency 1.2A (TG, p. 132) * ■ Transparency 1.2B (TG, p. 133) * ■ Labsheet 1.2 BLM (TG, p. 124)
Problem 1.3	1 day	8, 10, 11, 13, 15	■ Labsheet 1.3 (1 per pair) ■ paper clips or bobby pins (2 per pair)	■ Transparency 1.3A (TG, p. 134) * ■ Transparency 1.3B (TG, p. 135) * ■ Labsheet 1.3 BLM (TG, p. 125)
Problem 1.4 **Mathematical Reflections**	1 day	9, 12, 14, 16, 17, 19, 20 MR 1–3	 ■ journal	■ Transparency 1.4 (TG, p. 136) *

* optional materials

© Prentice-Hall, Inc.

Investigation 2: Analyzing Number-Cube Games

Mathematical and Problem-Solving Goals

- To review and develop a deeper understanding of experimental and theoretical probabilities and the relationship between them

- To review familiar methods of finding experimental and theoretical probabilities, including experimenting and making an organized list of possible outcomes

- To determine whether a game is fair and to find a way to change an unfair game to a fair game by informally applying the concept of expected value

Problems in this Investigation

Problem 2.1: Playing the Addition Game *(pages 22–23)*
Problem 2.2: Playing the Multiplication Game *(page 23)*

Resource Options for Planning

	Suggested Pacing	Assignment Guide (ACE questions)	Materials for Students	Resources for Teachers
Investigation 2	2 days total	Exercises are in Student Edition, pp. 24–30	■ graphing calculators ■ large sheets of paper *	■ Additional Practice, Investigation 2 (TG, p. 165)
Problem 2.1	1 day	1–6, 11–15, 18, 20–23	■ Labsheet 2.1 (1 per pair) * ■ number cubes (2 per pair)	■ Transparency 2.1 (TG, p. 137) * ■ Labsheet 2.1 BLM (TG, p. 126) *
Problem 2.2 **Mathematical Reflections**	1 day	7–10, 16, 17, 19, 24 MR 1–3	■ Labsheet 2.2 (1 per pair) * ■ number cubes (2 per pair) ■ journal	■ Transparency 2.2 (TG, p. 138) * ■ Labsheet 2.2 BLM (TG, p. 127) *

* optional materials

© Prentice-Hall, Inc.

Investigation 3: Probability and Area

Mathematical and Problem-Solving Goals

- To review and come to a deeper understanding of experimental and theoretical probabilities and the relationship between them

- To begin thinking about probabilities in terms of area on a grid as an introduction to the area model for analyzing probabilities

Problems in this Investigation

Problem 3.1: Cracking Level 1 *(pages 32–34)*
Problem 3.2: Cracking Level 2 *(pages 34–35)*

Resource Options for Planning

	Suggested Pacing	Assignment Guide (ACE questions)	Materials for Students	Resources for Teachers
Investigation 3	2 days total	Exercises are in Student Edition, pp. 36–39	■ graphing calculators	■ Additional Practice, Investigation 3 (TG, p. 166)
Problem 3.1	1 day	1, 5–8	■ computers * ■ Treasure Hunt program *	■ Transparency 3.1A (TG, p. 139) * ■ Transparency 3.1B (TG, p. 140) *
Problem 3.2	1 day	2–4, 9	■ grid paper *	■ Transparency 3.2A (TG, p. 141) * ■ Transparency 3.2B (TG, p. 142) * ■ Transparency 3.2C (TG, p. 143) *
Mathematical Reflections		MR 1, 2	■ journal	■ Grid paper BLM (TG, p. 162)

* optional materials

© Prentice-Hall, Inc.

Investigation 4: Analyzing Two-Stage Games

Mathematical and Problem-Solving Goals

■ To use an area model to represent the probability of two or more dependent events

■ To solve problems by determining the probabilities of two or more dependent events

Problems in this Investigation

Problem 4.1: Choosing Paths *(pages 41–43)*

Problem 4.2: Finding the Best Arrangement *(pages 43–44)*

Resource Options for Planning

	Suggested Pacing	Assignment Guide (ACE questions)	Materials for Students	Resources for Teachers
Investigation 4	3 days total	Exercises are in Student Edition pp. 45–48	■ graphing calculators ■ grid paper *	■ Additional Practice, Investigation 4 (TG, pp. 167–168) ■ transparent grids * ■ Grid paper BLM (TG, p. 162)
Problem 4.1	1 day	1, 4, 7	■ spinners ■ colored blocks ■ coins ■ number cubes	■ Transparency 4.1 (TG, p. 144) *
Problem 4.2	2 days	2, 3, 5, 6	■ colored blocks (2 of each of 2 colors per group) ■ opaque containers large enough for a student's hand (2 identical containers per group)	■ Transparency 4.2 (TG, p. 145) *
Mathematical Reflections		MR 1, 2	■ journal	

* optional materials

© Prentice-Hall, Inc.

Lesson Planner

Investigation 5: Expected Value

Mathematical and Problem-Solving Goals

- To determine the probability of an event that consists of a sequence of two independent outcomes in which the probability of the second outcome depends on the first outcome
- To understand how to use probabilities and equivalent fractions to find expected value
- To use area models and the concept of expected value to solve probability problems

Problems in this Investigation

Problem 5.1: Shooting the One-and-One *(pages 50–51)*
Problem 5.2: Finding Expected Value *(pages 51–52)*

Resource Options for Planning

	Suggested Pacing	Assignment Guide (ACE questions)	Materials for Students	Resources for Teachers
Investigation 5	3 days total	Exercises are in Student Edition, pp. 53–57	■ graphing calulators ■ 10 by 10 grids *	■ Additional Practice, Investigation 5 (TG, p. 169) ■ transparent 10 by 10 grid * ■ BLM for 10 by 10 grid (TG, p. 158) *
Problem 5.1	1 day	7–9	■ Labsheet 5.1 (1 per 2 pairs) * ■ colored blocks ■ 10-sided number cubes	■ Transparency 5.1A (TG, p. 146) * ■ Transparency 5.1B (TG, p. 147) * ■ Labsheet 5.1 BLM (TG, p. 128) *
Problem 5.2	2 days	1–6, 10–13	■ Labsheet 5.2 (1 per pair) * ■ 10-section, 12-section, and 16-section spinners *	■ Transparency 5.2 (TG, p. 148) * ■ transparency of Labsheet 5.2 * ■ Labsheet 5.2 BLM (TG, p. 129) * ■ BLM for 10-section, 12-section, and 16-section spinners (TG, pp. 159–161) *
Mathematical Reflections		MR 1, 2	■ journal	

* optional materials

© Prentice-Hall, Inc.

Investigation 6: Carnival Games

Mathematical and Problem-Solving Goals

- To find probabilities in situations that involve drawing with and without replacement
- To find and compare theoretical and experimental probabilities
- To use probability to compute expected value
- To use probability analysis to help make decisions

Problems in this Investigation

Problem 6.1: Drawing Marbles *(pages 59–60)*
Problem 6.2: Choosing the Best Game *(pages 60–61)*
Problem 6.3: Taking a Computer Safari *(pages 61–63)*

Resource Options for Planning

	Suggested Pacing	Assignment Guide (ACE questions)	Materials for Students	Resources for Teachers
Investigation 6	3 days total	Exercises are in Student Edition, pp. 64–67	■ graphing calculators	■ Additional Practice, Investigation 6 (TG, p. 170)
Problem 6.1	1 day	1–3	■ colored blocks (4 of one color and 1 of another per pair) ■ opaque containers large enough for a student's hand (1 per pair)	■ Transparency 6.1 (TG, p. 149) *
Problem 6.2	1 day	4–7	■ coins (1 per group of 2 or 3 students) ■ grid paper *	■ Transparency 6.2 (TG, p. 150) * ■ Grid paper BLM (TG, p. 162)
Problem 6.3	1 day	8–10		■ Transparency 6.3 (TG, p. 151) *
Mathematical Reflections		MR 1–2	■ journal	

* optional materials

© Prentice-Hall, Inc.

Investigation 7: Analyzing Sequences of Outcomes

Mathematical and Problem-Solving Goals

■ To use counting trees for finding theoretical probabilities in binomial, or 50–50, probability situations

■ To understand the distinction between specific outcomes and events composed of a sequence of outcomes

■ To recognize that simultaneous trials and trials conducted one at a time give the same information

■ To use expected value to help make decisions in probability situations

Problems in this Investigation

Problem 7.1: Counting Puppies *(pages 69–70)*
Problem 7.2: Guessing Answers *(pages 70–73)*

Resource Options for Planning

	Suggested Pacing	Assignment Guide (ACE questions)	Materials for Students	Resources for Teachers
Investigation 7	3 days total	Exercises are in Student Edition, pp. 74–77	■ graphing calculators	■ Additional Practice, Investigation 7 (TG, p. 171)
Problem 7.1	1 day	1–3, 7, 9, 10		■ Transparency 7.1 (TG, p. 152) *
Problem 7.2	2 days	4–6, 8, 11, 12	■ Labsheet 7.2 (1 per group) * ■ coins (1 per group)	■ Transparency 7.2A (TG, p. 153) * ■ Transparency 7.2B (TG, p. 154) * ■ transparency of Labsheet 7.2 * ■ Labsheet 7.2 BLM (TG, p. 130) *
Mathematical Reflections		MR 1–3	■ journal	

* optional materials

© Prentice-Hall, Inc.

Unit Organizer

Data Around Us

Pacing Options

Investigations and Assessments	Class Time (days)
1 Interpreting Disaster Reports (SE, pp. 5–11)	2
2 Measuring Oil Spills (SE, pp. 12–22)	3
3 Comparing Large Numbers (SE, pp. 23–37)	4
Check-Up (TG, p. 73)	1/2
4 How Many Is a Million? (SE, pp. 38–50)	3
5 Every Litter Bit Hurts (SE, pp. 51–60)	4
Quiz (TG, p. 74)	1/2
6 On an Average Day (SE, pp. 61–69)	3
Looking Back and Looking Ahead: Unit Reflections (SE, pp. 70–72)	1
Self-Assessment (TG, p. 81)	take home
Unit Test (TG, pp. 78–79)	1

Teacher's Guide and Ancillary Resources

Assessment Resources (pp. 71–91)

Blackline Masters (pp. 93–125)

Additional Practice (pp. 127–133)

 Assessment and Additional Practice

Essential Vocabulary

customary system

metric system, international system of measurement, SI system

million, billion, trillion

scientific notation

standard notation

Prerequisite Units

Shapes and Designs (Geometry, Measurement)

Stretching and Shrinking (Geometry, Measurement)

Comparing and Scaling (Number and Operations, Algebra)

Filling and Wrapping (Geometry, Measurement)

NCTM Principles and Standards 2000

Content Standard: Number and Operations, Measurement

Process Standards: Problem Solving, Reasoning and Proof, Communication, Connections, and Representation

Materials

Graphing calculators

Sets of base ten blocks (optional)

Unit cubes

Almanacs or U.S. maps

Stick-on notes

Yardsticks and metersticks (1 each per group)

Bobby pins or paper clips (1 per group)

Transparencies of Labsheets 3.1A, 3.2, and 4.2 (optional)

Overhead graphing or scientific calculator (optional)

Large U.S. map (optional)

Cardboard boxes with bases approximately 1-ft square or with dimensions that represent combinations of 1-ft square bases, such as 1 ft by 2 ft by 1 ft (optional)

Common objects to illustrate some units of measure, such as cup, pint, and quart containers; and foot rulers, yardsticks, and metersticks (optional)

Mathematics in the Unit

- Choose sensible units for measuring.
- Build a repertoire of benchmarks to relate unfamiliar things to things that are personally meaningful.
- Read, write, and interpret the large numbers that occur in real-life measurements using standard, scientific, and calculator notation.
- Review the concept of place value as it relates to reading, writing, and using large numbers.
- Review and extend the use of exponents.
- Use estimates and rounded values for describing and comparing objects and events.
- Assess the accuracy and reliability of numbers used to report information.
- Choose sensible ways of comparing counts and measurements, including using differences, rates, and ratios.
- Understand that a measurement has two components, a unit of measure and a count.

© Prentice-Hall, Inc.

Connections to Other Units

The ideas in *Data Around Us* build on and connect to several big ideas in other Connected Mathematics units.

Big Idea	Prior Work	Future Work
understanding and comparing large numbers	scaling quantities up or down; comparing quantities expressed in decimal, percent, or fraction form; comparing categorical and numerical data (*Data About Us; Bits and Pieces II; Comparing and Scaling; Filling and Wrapping*)	comparing growth rates and stages of exponential growth (*Growing, Growing, Growing*); making meaningful comparisons among data about populations (*Samples and Populations*)
choosing appropriate units of measure and understanding the notation used to express large numbers	choosing appropriate units for measuring distance, area, surface area, and volume (*Covering and Surrounding; Filling and Wrapping*); using exponents (*Prime Time*); selecting scales for graphs (*Variables and Patterns*)	analyzing data that describe attributes and behavior of large populations (*Samples and Populations*); using scientific notation (*Growing, Growing, Growing*)
estimating with large numbers	developing benchmarks for estimating with decimals, percents, and fractions (*Bits and Pieces I; Bits and Pieces II*); estimating populations based on population densities (*Comparing and Scaling; Filling and Wrapping*)	making inferences and predictions about large populations; developing strategies for estimating quantities based on analysis (*Samples and Populations; Clever Counting*)
calculating with large numbers	developing algorithms for performing calculations with fractions, decimals, and percents (*Bits and Pieces II*); applying ratios, proportions, and percents (*Comparing and Scaling*)	making predictions based on patterns of exponential growth or decay (*Growing, Growing, Growing*); making inferences and predictions about large populations (*Samples and Populations*); developing strategies for efficiently counting large numbers of objects or outcomes (*Clever Counting*)
determining population density	analyzing data about populations and groups (*Data About Us*); calculating and applying population densities (*Comparing and Scaling*)	using information about populations and exponential growth patterns to predict population doubling time and half life (*Growing, Growing, Growing*); using data about a sample of a population to draw informed conclusions and make inferences about the entire population (*Samples and Populations*)

© Prentice-Hall, Inc.

Lesson Planner

Investigation 1: Interpreting Disaster Reports

Mathematical and Problem-Solving Goals

■ To consider some of the issues related to working with large numbers, including accuracy of reported numbers, methods of determining reported measures, and language used to make numerical comparisons

■ To review operations with large numbers

Problems in this Investigation

Problem 1.1: Comparing Disasters *(pages 5–6)*

Problem 1.2: Aiding Hurricane Victims *(pages 7–8)*

Resource Options for Planning

	Suggested Pacing	Assignment Guide (ACE questions)	Materials for Students	Resources for Teachers
Investigation 1	2 days total	Exercises are in Student Edition, pp. 9–10	■ graphing calculators	■ Additional Practice, Investigation 1 (TG, p. 128) ■ overhead graphing calculator *
Problem 1.1	1 day	1–6		■ Transparency 1.1A (TG, p. 99) * ■ Transparency 1.1B (TG, p. 100) *
Problem 1.2	1 day	7–9	■ yardsticks (1 or more) ■ blank transparencies * ■ almanacs	■ Transparency 1.2A (TG, p. 101) * ■ Transparency 1.2B (TG, p. 102) *
Mathematical Reflections		MR 1, 2	■ journal	

* optional materials

© Prentice-Hall, Inc.

Investigation 2: Measuring Oil Spills

Mathematical and Problem-Solving Goals

- To revisit the ways that numbers are used in measurement to describe objects and events

- To begin building a repertoire of measurement benchmarks for use in relating measurement information to things that are personally meaningful

- To develop skill in using benchmark strategies, such as comparing a given figure to multiple copies of a more familiar object

Problems in this Investigation

Problem 2.1: Describing an Oil Spill *(pages 12–13)*

Problem 2.2: Finding Benchmarks for Units of Measure *(pages 14–15)*

Problem 2.3: Developing a Sense of Large Numbers *(pages 16–18)*

Resource Options for Planning

	Suggested Pacing	Assignment Guide (ACE questions)	Materials for Students	Resources for Teachers
Investigation 2	3 days total	Exercises are in Student Edition, pp. 19–21	■ graphing calculators	■ Additional Practice, Investigation 2 (TG, p. 129)
Problem 2.1	1 day	1, 9–11	■ Labsheet 2.1 (1 per pair) *	■ Transparency 2.1 (TG, p. 103) ■ Labsheet 2.1 BLM (TG, p. 94)
Problem 2.2	1 day	8	■ yardsticks (1 per group) ■ stick-on notes (several per student)	■ Transparency 2.2 (TG, p. 104) ■ common objects to illustrate some units of measure, such as cup, pint, and quart containers; and foot rulers, yardsticks, and metersticks *
Problem 2.3	1 day	2–7	■ blank transparencies or large sheets of paper *	■ Transparency 2.3A (TG, p. 105) ■ Transparency 2.3B (TG, p. 106) ■ almanacs or atlases
Mathematical Reflections		MR 1–3	■ journal	

* optional materials

© Prentice-Hall, Inc.

Investigation 3: Comparing Large Numbers

Mathematical and Problem-Solving Goals

- To read and write large numbers
- To round numbers and to make judgments about the degree of accuracy of numbers
- To compare large numbers by ordering and with rates

Problems in this Investigation

Problem 3.1: Playing Dialing Digits *(pages 24–25)*

Problem 3.2: Getting Things in Order *(pages 25–27)*

Problem 3.3: Rounding Numbers *(page 28)*

Problem 3.4: Comparing Hog Populations *(pages 29–30)*

Resource Options for Planning

	Suggested Pacing	Assignment Guide (ACE questions)	Materials for Students	Resources for Teachers
Investigation 3	4 days total	Exercises are in Student Edition, pp. 31–36	■ graphing calculators	■ Additional Practice, Investigation 3 (TG, p. 130)
Problem 3.1	1 day	1, 2, 8, 12	■ Labsheet 3.1A (1 per pair or group) ■ Labsheet 3.1B (1 per student or pair) ■ bobby pins or paper clips (1 per group)	■ Transparency 3.1 (TG, p. 107) * ■ Labsheets 3.1A and 3.1B BLM (TG, pp. 95–96) ■ transparency of Labsheet 3.1A *
Problem 3.2	1 day	3, 4, 11	■ Labsheet 3.2 (1 per group) ■ almanacs or U.S. maps	■ Transparency 3.2A (TG, p. 108) * ■ Transparency 3.2B (TG, p. 109) * ■ Transparency 3.2C (TG, p. 110) * ■ Labsheet 3.2 BLM (TG, p. 97) ■ transparency of Labsheet 3.2 * ■ large U.S. map *
Problem 3.3	1 day	6, 7, 9, 13, 16–19		■ Transparency 3.3 (TG, p. 111) *
Problem 3.4	1 day	5, 10, 14, 15		■ Transparency 3.4 (TG, p. 112) *
Mathematical Reflections		MR 1–3	■ journal	

* optional materials

© Prentice-Hall, Inc.

Lesson Planner

Investigation 4: How Many Is a Million?

Mathematical and Problem-Solving Goals

■ To build a concrete understanding of a million in a variety of contexts

■ To review and extend the concept of place value as it relates to reading, writing, and using large numbers

■ To review and extend the use of exponents

■ To write and interpret large numbers using scientific and calculator notation

■ To estimate with large numbers

Problems in this Investigation

Problem 4.1: Thinking Big *(pages 38–39)*

Problem 4.2: Thinking Even Bigger *(pages 39–40)*

Problem 4.3: Using Scientific Notation *(pages 41–43)*

Resource Options for Planning

	Suggested Pacing	Assignment Guide (ACE questions)	Materials for Students	Resources for Teachers
Investigation 4	3 days total	Exercises are in Student Edition, pp. 44–49	■ graphing calculators	■ Additional Practice, Investigation 4 (TG, p. 131)
Problem 4.1	1 day	1–3	■ metersticks (1 per group)	■ Transparency 4.1 (TG, p. 113) *
Problem 4.2	1 day	4, 5, 11–13, 17, 20	■ Labsheet 4.2 * ■ sets of base ten blocks * ■ unit cubes	■ Transparency 4.2A (TG, p. 114) * ■ Transparency 4.2B (TG, p. 115) * ■ transparency of Labsheet 4.2 * ■ Labsheet 4.2 BLM (TG, p. 98)
Problem 4.3 **Mathematical Reflections**	1 day	6–10, 14–16, 18, 19 MR 1–4	 ■ journal	■ Transparency 4.3 (TG, p. 116) * ■ overhead graphing calculator *

* optional materials

© Prentice-Hall, Inc.

Lesson Planner

Investigation 5: Every Litter Bit Hurts

Mathematical and Problem-Solving Goals

■ To further develop operation sense, the ability to choose the numbers and operations needed to answer specific questions from given information

■ To investigate how small quantities can accumulate to produce a large quantity

Problems in this Investigation

Problem 5.1: Going Hog Wild *(pages 51–52)*

Problem 5.2: Recycling Cans *(pages 52–53)*

Problem 5.3: Going Down the Drain *(page 53)*

Problem 5.4: Making Mountains out of Molehills *(page 54)*

Resource Options for Planning

	Suggested Pacing	Assignment Guide (ACE questions)	Materials for Students	Resources for Teachers
Investigation 5	4 days total	Exercises are in Student Edition, pp. 55–59	■ graphing calculators	■ Additional Practice, Investigation 5 (TG, p. 132)
Problem 5.1	1 day	4, 6–8		■ Transparency 5.1 (TG, p. 117) *
Problem 5.2	1 day	1, 2, 5		■ Transparency 5.2 (TG, p. 118) *
Problem 5.3	1 day	3		■ Transparency 5.3 (TG, p. 119) *
Problem 5.4	1 day	9, 10	■ yardsticks (1 per group) ■ atlases or almanacs	■ Transparency 5.4 (TG, p. 120) * ■ cardboard boxes with bases approximately 1-ft square or with dimensions that represent combinations of 1-ft square bases *
Mathematical Reflections		MR 1, 2	■ journal	

* optional materials

© Prentice-Hall, Inc.

Investigation 6: On an Average Day

Mathematical and Problem-Solving Goals

- To make decisions about the best way to compare quantities

- To apply various strategies for writing and comparing quantities

- To use appropriate benchmarks to make sense of large numbers

Problems in this Investigation

Problem 6.1: Recycling Cans *(page 61)*

Problem 6.2: Making Comparisons in Two Ways *(page 62)*

Problem 6.3: Comparing by Using Rates *(page 63)*

Resource Options for Planning

	Suggested Pacing	Assignment Guide (ACE questions)	Materials for Students	Resources for Teachers
Investigation 6	3 days total	Exercises are in Student Edition pp. 64–68	■ graphing calculators	■ Additional Practice, Investigation 6 (TG, p. 133)
Problem 6.1	1 day	10, 14–17		■ Transparency 6.1 (TG, p. 121) *
Problem 6.2	1 day	1–4		■ Transparency 6.2 (TG, p. 122) *
Problem 6.3	1 day	5–9, 11–13	■ atlases	■ Transparency 6.3 (TG, p. 123) *
Mathematical Reflections		MR 1–3	■ journal	

* optional materials

© Prentice-Hall, Inc.

Thinking with Mathematical Models

Pacing Options

Investigations and Assessments	Class Time (days)
1 Linear Models (SE, pp. 5–25)	6
Check-Up (TG, pp. 63–64)	1/2
2 Nonlinear Models (SE, pp. 26–36)	4
Quiz (TG, pp. 65–66)	1
3 More Nonlinear Models (SE, pp. 37–46)	3
4 A World of Patterns (SE, pp. 47–59)	4
Looking Back and Looking Ahead: Unit Reflections (SE, pp. 60–62)	1
Self-Assessment (TG, p. 73)	take home
Unit Test (TG, pp. 69–71)	1

Teacher's Guide and Ancillary Resources

Assessment Resources (pp. 61–90)

Blackline Masters (pp. 91–113)

Additional Practice (pp. 115–125)

 Assessment and Additional Practice

Essential Vocabulary

equation model

fulcrum

graph model

inverse relationship

linear relationship

mathematical model

relationship

Prerequisite Units

Variables and Patterns (Algebra)

Accentuate the Negative (Number and Operations)

Moving Straight Ahead (Algebra)

NCTM Principles and Standards 2000

Content Standard: Algebra

Process Standards: Problem Solving, Reasoning and Proof, Communication, Connections, and Representation

Materials

Graphing calculators (preferably with the capacity to display a function as a table)

11" by 4" strips of paper (about 15 per group)

4" strips of paper cut to lengths of 4" to 11" plus extra 4" by 11" strips for cutting to length as needed (see Problem 2.1)

Blocks of wood or cardboard fulcrums (1 per group)

Weights such as heavy washers (about 20 per group) or pennies (about 80 per group)

Small paper cups (3-oz size works well)

Metersticks (1 per group)

8 identical clear drinking glasses

Water

Food coloring (optional)

Stick-on notes or masking tape

Mathematics in the Unit

- Develop skill in collecting data from experiments and systematically recording that data in tables.
- Construct coordinate graphs to represent data.
- Make predictions from data tables or graph models.
- Use patterns in data to find equations that model relationships between variables.
- Use tables, graphs, and equations to model linear and nonlinear relationships between variables.
- Distinguish between linear and nonlinear relationships.
- Identify inverse relationships and describe their characteristics.
- Use a graphing calculator to find and study graph models and equation models of relationships between variables.
- Use intuitive ideas about rates of change to sketch graphs for, and to match graphs to, given situations.
- Use intuitive ideas about rates of change to create stories that fit given graphs.

© Prentice-Hall, Inc.

Connections to Other Units

The ideas in *Thinking with Mathematical Models* build on and connect to several big ideas in other Connected Mathematics units.

Big Idea	Prior Work	Future Work
building and analyzing mathematical models	generalizing formulas *(Covering and Surrounding; Filling and Wrapping)*; using symbols to represent relationships *(Variables and Patterns; Moving Straight Ahead)*; making tables and graphs by hand and with a graphing calculator *(Data About Us; How Likely Is It?; Accentuate the Negative; Moving Straight Ahead)*	recognizing families of functions *(Growing, Growing, Growing; Frogs, Fleas, and Painted Cubes)*; manipulating symbols to find alternative forms of expression and to solve linear equations *(Say It with Symbols)*; recognizing patterns of growth and change from tables and graph models *(Growing, Growing, Growing; Frogs, Fleas, and Painted Cubes)*
fitting a line to experimental data	writing the equation of a line from information about its slope and points on the line *(Moving Straight Ahead)*	fitting lines and making predictions *(Samples and Populations)*
identifying the variables of interest in a situation	identifying dependent and independent variables and observing how change in the dependent variable is related to change in the independent variable *(Variables and Patterns; Accentuate the Negative; Moving Straight Ahead)*	determining patterns of growth in different kinds of equations *(Growing, Growing, Growing; Frogs, Fleas, and Painted Cubes)*
conducting experiments to gather data about how variables are related	conducting experiments involving linear relationships *(Data About Us; Variables and Patterns; Moving Straight Ahead)*	conducting experiments involving exponential and quadratic relationships *(Growing, Growing, Growing; Frogs, Fleas, and Painted Cubes)*

© Prentice-Hall, Inc.

Lesson Planner

Investigation 1: Linear Models

Mathematical and Problem-Solving Goals

- To collect data, record data in tables, and represent data in coordinate graphs
- To fit a linear model to a graph
- To make predictions from data tables and graph models
- To write an equation given the graph of a line
- To review the meaning of slope and *y*-intercept in relation to a set of data
- To write the equation of a line given the slope and the *y*-intercept, the slope and the coordinates of a point on the line, or the coordinates of two points on the line

Problems in this Investigation

Problem 1.1: Testing Paper Bridges *(pages 5–6)*
Problem 1.2: Drawing Graph Models *(pages 7–8)*
Problem 1.3: Finding Equation Models *(pages 9–10)*
Problem 1.4: Setting the Right Price *(pages 10–12)*
Problem 1.5: Writing Equations for Lines *(pages 12–14)*

Resource Options for Planning

	Suggested Pacing	Assignment Guide (ACE questions)	Materials for Students	Resources for Teachers
Investigation 1	6 days total	Exercises are in Student Edition, pp. 15–24	■ grId paper ■ graphing calculators ■ calculator grids	■ Grid paper BLM (TG, p. 112) ■ Calculator grids BLM (TG, p. 113) ■ Additional Practice, Investigation 1 (TG, pp. 116–117)
Problem 1.1	1 day	29–31	■ 11" by 4" strips of paper (15 per group) ■ small paper cups ■ pennies (50 per group) ■ chalk or masking tape * ■ blank transparencies *	■ Transparency 1.1 (TG, p. 94) *
Problem 1.2	1 day	25, 28	■ Labsheet 1.2 (1 per student) ■ transparent grids or blank transparencies *	■ Transparency 1.2A (TG, p. 95) * ■ Transparency 1.2B (TG, p. 96) * ■ Labsheet 1.2 BLM (TG, p. 92) ■ transparency of Labsheet 1.2 *
Problem 1.3	1 day	1, 4–8, 26, 40, 41	■ blank transparencies *	■ overhead graphing calculator * ■ Transparency 1.3 (TG, p. 97) *
Problem 1.4	1 day	2, 3, 24, 27, 39	■ transparent grids *	■ Transparency 1.4 (TG, p. 98) *
Problem 1.5	2 days	9–23, 32–38		■ Transparency 1.5A (TG, p. 99) * ■ Transparency 1.5B (TG, p. 100) *
Mathematical Reflections		MR 1–5	■ journal	

* optional materials

© Prentice-Hall, Inc.

Investigation 2: Nonlinear Models

Mathematical and Problem-Solving Goals

■ To express data in tables and graphs

■ To make predictions from tables and graph models

■ To distinguish between linear and nonlinear relationships

■ To identify inverse relationships and describe their characteristics

Problems in this Investigation

Problem 2.1: Testing Bridge Lengths *(pages 26–27)*

Problem 2.2: Keeping Things Balanced *(pages 28–29)*

Problem 2.3: Testing Whether Driving Fast Pays *(page 30)*

Resource Options for Planning

	Suggested Pacing	Assignment Guide (ACE questions)	Materials for Students	Resources for Teachers
Investigation 2	4 days total	Exercises are in Student Edition, pp. 31–35	■ grid paper ■ graphing calculators ■ calculator grids	■ Calculator grids BLM (TG, p. 113) ■ Grid paper BLM (TG, p. 112) ■ Additional Practice, Investigation 2 (TG, pp. 118–119)
Problem 2.1	1 day	8, 9	■ 4″ strips of pater cut to lengths of 4″ to 11″ plus extra strips to cut to length as needed ■ small paper cups ■ pennies (50 per group) ■ chalk or masking tape * ■ large sheets of paper *	■ Transparency 2.1A (TG, p. 101) * ■ Transparency 2.1B (TG, p. 102) *
Problem 2.2	1 day	3–7	■ weights such as heavy washers (20 per group) or pennies (80 per group) ■ blocks of wood or cardboard fulcrums (1 per group) ■ metersticks (1 per group) ■ large sheets of paper *	■ Transparency 2.2A (TG, p. 103) *
Problem 2.3	2 days	1, 2, 10–12	■ large sheets of paper *	■ Transparency 2.3 (TG, p. 104) *
Mathematical Reflections		MR 1–3	■ journal	

* optional materials

© Prentice-Hall, Inc.

Investigation 3: More Nonlinear Models

Mathematical and Problem-Solving Goals

■ To use knowledge about percents and fractions to generate data

■ To explore a new type of graph model and to compare it to those explored previously

■ To use a graph model to make predictions

■ To continue to develop the idea of using a graph to model the trend in a data set

Problems in this Investigation

Problem 3.1: Earning Interest *(pages 37–39)*

Problem 3.2: Pouring Water *(pages 39–40)*

Resource Options for Planning

	Suggested Pacing	Assignment Guide (ACE questions)	Materials for Students	Resources for Teachers
Investigation 3	3 days total	Exercises are in Student Edition, pp. 41–45	■ grid paper ■ graphing calculators	■ Grid paper BLM (TG, p. 112) ■ Calculator grids BLM (TG, p. 113) ■ Additional Practice, Investigation 3 (TG, pp. 120–122)
Problem 3.1	1 day	1, 3, 5	■ blank transparencies or large sheets of paper *	■ Transparency 3.1 (TG, p. 105) *
Problem 3.2	2 days	2, 4, 6, 7	■ Labsheet 3.ACE (1 per student)	■ Transparency 3.2 (TG, p. 106) * ■ Labsheet 3.ACE BLM (TG, p. 93) ■ 8 indentical clear drinking glasses ■ water ■ food coloring *
Mathematical Reflections		MR 1–4	■ journal	■ stick-on notes or masking tape

* optional materials

© Prentice-Hall, Inc.

Lesson Planner

Investigation 4: A World of Patterns

Mathematical and Problem-Solving Goals

■ To use intuitive ideas about rates of change to sketch graphs for, and to match graphs to, given situations

■ To use intuitive ideas about rates of change to create stories that fit given graphs

■ To extend understanding of graph models to include new shapes

■ To explore symbolic representations for several graph models

Problems in this Investigation

Problem 4.1: Modeling Real-Life Events *(pages 47–49)*

Problem 4.2: Writing Stories to Match Graphs *(pages 49–50)*

Problem 4.3: Exploring Graphs *(page 51)*

Resource Options for Planning

	Suggested Pacing	Assignment Guide (ACE questions)	Materials for Students	Resources for Teachers
Investigation 1	4 days total	Exercises are in Student Edition, pp. 52–58	■ grid paper ■ graphing calculators	■ overhead graphing calculator* ■ Grid paper BLM (TG, p. 112) ■ Calculator grids BLM (TG, p. 113) ■ Additional Practice, Investigation 4 (TG, pp. 123–125)
Problem 4.1	1 day	1–4, 6–8		■ Transparency 4.1 (TG, p. 107) *
Problem 4.2	1 day	5, 9	■ blank transparencies *	■ Transparency 4.2 (TG, p. 108) *
Problem 4.3	2 days	10	■ paper or transparent graphing calculator grids *	■ Transparency 4.3 (TG, p. 109) *
Mathematical Reflections		MR 1–3	■ journal	

* optional materials

© Prentice-Hall, Inc.

Looking for Pythagoras

Pacing Options

Investigations and Assessments	Class Time (days)
1 Locating Points (SE, pp. 5–16)	4
2 Finding Areas and Lengths (SE, pp. 17–26)	4
Check-Up (TG, pp. 76–77)	1/2
3 The Pythagorean Theorem (SE, pp. 27–40)	5
4 Using the Pythagorean Theorem (SE, pp. 41–52)	4
Quiz (TG, pp. 78–79)	1
5 Irrational Numbers (SE, pp. 53–63)	4
6 Rational and Irrational Slopes (SE, pp. 64–72)	3
Looking Back and Looking Ahead: Unit Reflections (SE, pp. 73–75)	1
Self-Assessment (TG, p. 88)	take home
Unit Test (TG, pp. 85–86)	1

Teacher's Guide and Ancillary Resources

Assessment Resources (pp. 75–96)

Blackline Masters (pp. 97–136)

Additional Practice (pp. 137–148)

 Assessment and Additional Practice

Essential Vocabulary

hypotenuse	repeating decimal
irrational number	square root
perpendicular	terminating
Pythagorean Theorem	decimal
rational number	
real numbers	

Prerequisite Units

None

NCTM Principles and Standards 2000

Content Standard: Number and Operations, Algebra, Geometry, and Measurement

Process Standards: Problem Solving, Reasoning and Proof, Communication, Connections, and Representation

Materials

Graphing calculators

Geoboards (optional)

Dot paper

String or straws

Centimeter rulers (1 per student)

Scissors

Transparencies of Labsheets (optional)

Transparent dot paper (optional)

Transparent centimeter grid (optional)

Overhead geoboard (optional)

Mathematics in the Unit

- Understand relationships between coordinates, slope, distance, and area.
- Relate the area of a square to the length of a side.
- Develop strategies for finding the distance between two dots on a dot grid or two points on a coordinate grid.
- Discover and apply the Pythagorean Theorem
- Extend understanding of number systems to include irrational numbers.
- Locate irrational numbers on a number line.
- Represent fractions as decimals and decimals as fractions.
- Determine whether the decimal representation for a fraction terminates or repeats.
- Use slopes to solve interesting problems.

© Prentice-Hall, Inc.

Connections to Other Units

The ideas in *Looking for Pythagoras* build on and connect to several big ideas in
other Connected Mathematics units.

Big Idea	Prior Work	Future Work
calculating the distance between two points in the plane	measuring lengths *(Shapes and Designs; Covering and Surrounding)*; working with coordinates *(Variables and Patterns; Moving Straight Ahead; Thinking with Mathematical Models)*	finding midpoints of line segments *(Hubcaps, Kaleidoscopes, and Mirrors)*
finding areas of figures drawn on a coordinate grid with whole-number vertices	measuring areas of polygons and irregular figures *(Covering and Surrounding; Bits and Pieces I)*	studying transformations and symmetries of plane figures *(Hubcaps, Kaleidoscopes, and Mirrors)*
understanding square roots as lengths of sides of squares	applying the formula for area of a square *(Covering and Surrounding)*	looking for patterns in square numbers *(Frogs, Fleas, and Painted Cubes)*
understanding the Pythagorean Theorem and how it relates the areas of the squares on the sides of a right triangle	formulating, reading, and interpreting symbolic rules *(Variables and Patterns; Moving Straight Ahead; Thinking with Mathematical Models)*; working with the triangle inequality *(Shapes and Designs)*	formulating and using symbolic rules and the syntax for manipulating symbols *(Frogs, Fleas, and Painted Cubes; Say It with Symbols)*
using the Pythagorean Theorem to solve problems	solving problems in geometric and algebraic contexts *(Shapes and Designs; Moving Straight Ahead; Thinking with Mathematical Models)*	solving geometric and algebraic problems *(Frogs, Fleas, and Painted Cubes; Say It with Symbols; Hubcaps, Kaleidoscopes, and Mirrors)*
investigating rational numbers written as decimals	understanding fractions and decimals *(Bits and Pieces I; Bits and Pieces II)*	exploring sampling and approximations *(Samples and Populations)*
understanding irrational numbers as nonterminating, nonrepeating decimals	representing fractions as decimals and decimals as fractions *(Bits and Pieces I; Bits and Pieces II)*	solving quadratic equations *(Frogs, Fleas, and Painted Cubes; Say It with Symbols)*
understanding slope relationships of perpendicular and parallel lines	finding slopes of lines and investigating parallel lines *(Variables and Patterns; Moving Straight Ahead)*	investigating symmetry *(Hubcaps, Kaleidoscopes, and Mirrors)*

© Prentice-Hall, Inc.

Lesson Planner

Investigation 1: Locating Points

Mathematical and Problem-Solving Goals

- To review the use of coordinates for specifying locations

- To use coordinates to specify direction and distance

- To connect properties of geometric shapes, such as parallel sides, to coordinate representations

Problems in this Investigation

Problem 1.1: Driving Around Euclid *(pages 8–9)*

Problem 1.2: Planning Emergency Routes *(pages 9–10)*

Problem 1.3: Planning Parks *(pages 10–11)*

Resource Options for Planning

	Suggested Pacing	Assignment Guide (ACE questions)	Materials for Students	Resources for Teachers
Investigation 1	4 days total	Exercises are in Student Edition, pp. 12–15	■ graphing calculators	■ Additional Practice, Investigation 1 (TG, pp. 138–139)
Problem 1.1	1 day	1, 3, 4, 7, 8		■ Transparency 1.1A (TG, p. 112) * ■ Transparency 1.1B (TG, p. 113) *
Problem 1.2	1 day	2, 9–11	■ centimeter rulers (1 per student)	■ Transparency 1.2 (TG, p. 114) * ■ transparent centimeter ruler *
Problem 1.3	2 days	5, 6, 12, 13	■ Labsheet 1.3 (1 per student) ■ centimeter grid paper ■ centimeter rulers *	■ Transparency 1.3 (TG, p. 115) * ■ transparency of Labsheet 1.3 * ■ Labsheet 1.3 BLM (TG, p. 98) ■ Centimeter grid paper BLM (TG, p. 136) ■ transparent grid *
Mathematical Reflections		MR 1–3	■ journal	

* optional materials

© Prentice-Hall, Inc.

Lesson Planner

Investigation 2: Finding Areas and Lengths

Mathematical and Problem-Solving Goals

■ To find areas of polygons drawn on a dot grid using various strategies

■ To find the length of a line segment drawn on a grid by thinking of it as the side of a square

■ To begin to develop an understanding of the concept of square root

Problems in this Investigation

Problem 2.1: Finding Areas *(pages 17–18)*

Problem 2.2: Looking for Squares *(pages 18–19)*

Problem 2.3: Finding Lengths *(pages 20–21)*

Resource Options for Planning

	Suggested Pacing	Assignment Guide (ACE questions)	Materials for Students	Resources for Teachers
Investigation 2	4 days total	Exercises are in Student Edition, pp. 22–25	■ graphing calculators	■ Additional Practice, Investigation 2 (TG, pp. 140–141) ■ overhead geoboard *
Problem 2.1	1 day	1, 3, 8, 9, 13, 14	■ Labsheet 2.1 ■ dot paper or geoboards (1 per pair) ■ Labsheet 2.ACE (1 per student) *	■ Transparency 2.1 (TG, p. 116) * ■ transparency of Labsheet 2.1 * ■ Labsheet 2.1 BLM (TG, p. 99) ■ transparent dot paper * ■ Dot paper BLM (TG, p. 135) ■ Labsheet 2.ACE BLM (TG, p. 102)
Problem 2.2	1 day	4, 6, 7, 11, 15	■ Labsheet 2.2 (1 per student) ■ centimeter rulers (1 per student) ■ Labsheet 2. ACE (1 per student)	■ Transparency 2.2 (TG, p. 117) * ■ Labsheet 2.2 BLM (TG, p. 100) ■ Labsheet 2.ACE BLM (TG, p. 102)
Problem 2.3	2 days	2, 5, 10, 12	■ Labsheet 2.3 (1 per student) ■ centimeter rulers (1 per student) ■ dot paper or geoboards * ■ Labsheet 2. ACE (1 per student)	■ Transparency 2.3 (TG, p. 118) * ■ Dot paper BLM (TG, p. 135) ■ Labsheet 2.3 BLM (TG, p. 101) ■ Labsheet 2.ACE BLM (TG, p. 102)
Mathematical Reflections		MR 1–3	■ journal	

* optional materials

© Prentice-Hall, Inc.

Lesson Planner

Investigation 3: The Pythagorean Theorem

Mathematical and Problem-Solving Goals

- To deduce the Pythagorean Theorem through exploration
- To use the Pythagorean Theorem to find areas of squares drawn on a dot grid
- To use the Pythagorean Theorem to find the distance between two points on a grid
- To determine whether a triangle is a right triangle
- To relate areas of squares to the lengths of the sides

Problems in this Investigation

Problem 3.1: Discovering the Pythagorean Theorem *(pages 27–28)*
Problem 3.2: Puzzling Through a Proof *(pages 29–30)*
Problem 3.3: Finding Distances *(page 31)*
Problem 3.4: Measuring the Egyptian Way *(pages 32–33)*

Resource Options for Planning

	Suggested Pacing	Assignment Guide (ACE questions)	Materials for Students	Resources for Teachers
Investigation 3	5 days total	Exercises are in Student Edition, pp. 34–39	■ graphing calculators	■ Additional Practice, Investigation 3 (TG, pp. 142–144)
Problem 3.1	1 day	3–7, 12, 13, 17, 18	■ dot paper	■ Transparency 3.1 (TG, p. 119) * ■ Dot paper BLM (TG, p. 135)
Problem 3.2	1 day	8–11, 20	■ Labsheets 3.2A, 3.2B and 3.2C (1 of each per student) ■ scissors	■ Transparency 3.2 (TG, p. 120) * ■ Labsheets 3.2A, 3.2B and 3.2C BLM (TG, pp. 103–105) ■ puzzle pieces and frames cut from transparencies of Labsheets 3.2A, 3.2B, and 3.2C *
Problem 3.3	1 day	1, 2, 19, 21–26	■ Labsheet 3.3 (1 per student) ■ dot paper	■ Transparency 3.3 (TG, p. 121) * ■ Dot paper BLM (TG, p. 135) ■ transparent grid * ■ Centimeter grid paper BLM (TG, p. 136) * ■ Labsheet 3.3 BLM (TG, p. 106)
Problem 3.4	2 days	14–16, 27	■ string or straws ■ rulers ■ scissors	■ Transparency 3.4A (TG, p. 122) * ■ Transparency 3.4B (TG, p. 123) * ■ transparent grid * ■ Centimeter grid paper BLM (TG, p. 136) *
Mathematical Reflections		MR 1–3	■ journal	

* optional materials

© Prentice-Hall, Inc.

Lesson Planner

Investigation 4: Using the Pythagorean Theorem

Mathematical and Problem-Solving Goals

- To apply the Pythagorean Theorem in several problem situations
- To investigate the special properties of a 30-60-90 right triangle
- To use the properties of special right triangles to solve problems

Problems in this Investigation

Problem 4.1: Stopping Sneaky Sally *(pages 41–42)*

Problem 4.2: Analyzing Triangles *(pages 43–44)*

Problem 4.3: Finding the Perimeter *(page 45)*

Resource Options for Planning

	Suggested Pacing	Assignment Guide (ACE questions)	Materials for Students	Resources for Teachers
Investigation 1	4 days total	Exercises are in Student Edition, pp. 46–51	■ graphing calculators	■ Additional Practice, Investigation 4 (TE, pp. 145–146)
Problem 4.1	1 day	1, 3, 5, 6	■ dot paper	■ Transparency 4.1 (TE, p. 124) * ■ transparent dot paper ■ Dot paper BLM (TE, p. 135)
Problem 4.2	1 day	2, 4, 7, 10	■ Labsheet 4.2 (1 per pair) ■ scissors	■ Transparency 4.2 (TE, p. 125) * ■ transparency of Labsheet 4.2 * ■ Labsheet 4.2 BLM (TE, p. 107)
Problem 4.3	2 days	8, 9, 11, 12		■ Transparency 4.3 (TE, p. 126) *
Mathematical Reflections		MR 1, 2	■ journal	

* optional materials

© Prentice-Hall, Inc.

Investigation 5: Irrational Numbers

Mathematical and Problem-Solving Goals

- To connect decimal and fractional representations of rational numbers
- To estimate lengths of hypotenuses of right triangles
- To explore patterns in terminating and repeating decimals

Problems in this Investigation

Problem 5.1: Analyzing the Wheel of Theodorus *(pages 54–55)*

Problem 5.2: Representing Fractions as Decimals *(page 56)*

Problem 5.3: Exploring Repeating Decimals *(pages 57–58)*

Resource Options for Planning

	Suggested Pacing	Assignment Guide (ACE questions)	Materials for Students	Resources for Teachers
Investigation 5	4 days total	Exercises are in Student Edition, pp. 59–62	■ graphing calculators	■ Additional Practice, Investigation 5 (TG, p. 147)
Problem 5.1	1 day	9–20	■ Labsheet 5.1 (1 per student) ■ scissors	■ Transparency 5.1 (TG, p. 127) * ■ transparency of Labsheet 5.1* ■ Labsheet 5.1 BLM, (TG, p. 108)
Problem 5.2	1 day	1–4, 21–24		■ Transparency 5.2 (TG, p. 128) *
Problem 5.3	2 days	5–8, 25–31		■ Transparency 5.3 (TG, p. 129) *
Mathematical Reflections		MR 1–5	■ journal	

* optional materials

© Prentice-Hall, Inc.

Investigation 6: Rational and Irrational Slopes

Mathematical and Problem-Solving Goals

- To review the concept of the slope of a line
- To connect the concept of slope to the idea of irrational numbers
- To use slopes to test whether lines are parallel or perpendicular

Problems in this Investigation

Problem 6.1: Revisiting Slopes *(pages 65–66)*

Problem 6.2: Escaping from the Forest *(pages 66–67)*

Resource Options for Planning

	Suggested Pacing	Assignment Guide (ACE questions)	Materials for Students	Resources for Teachers
Investigation 6	3 days total	Exercises are in Student Edition, pp. 68–71	■ graphing calculators	■ Additional Practice, Investigation 6 (TG, p. 148)
Problem 6.1	1 day	1–6, 8, 9, 15	■ Labsheet 6.ACE1 (1 per student) * ■ dot paper	■ Transparency 6.1A (TG, p. 130) * ■ Transparency 6.1B (TG, p. 131) * ■ Dot paper BLM (TG, p. 135) ■ Labsheet 6.ACE1 BLM (TG, p. 110)
Problem 6.2	2 days	7, 10–14, 16	■ Labsheet 6.2 (1 per student) ■ Labsheet 6.ACE2 (1 per student) ■ dot paper	■ Transparency 6.2 (TG, p. 132) * ■ transparency of dot paper * ■ Dot paper BLM (TG, p. 135) ■ Labsheet 6.2 BLM (TG, p. 109) ■ Labsheet 6.ACE2 BLM (TG, p. 111)
Mathematical Reflections		MR 1–5	■ journal	

* optional materials

© Prentice-Hall, Inc.

Unit Organizer

Growing, Growing, Growing

Pacing Options

Investigations and Assessments	Class Time (days)
1 Exponential Growth (SE, pp. 5–16)	4
2 Growth Patterns (SE, pp. 17–30)	4
Check-Up (TG, pp. 65–66)	1/2
3 Growth Factors (SE, pp. 31–44)	4
Quiz (TG, pp. 67–68)	1
4 Exponential Decay (SE, pp. 45–60)	5
Looking Back and Looking Ahead: Unit Reflections (SE, pp. 63–64)	1
Self-Assessment (TG, p. 79)	take home
Unit Test (TG, pp. 74–77)	1
Unit Project (SE, pp. 61–62, optional)	1–2

Teacher's Guide and Ancillary Resources

Assessment Resources (pp. 63–93)

Blackline Masters (pp. 95–118)

Additional Practice (pp. 119–127)

Assessment and Additional Practice

Essential Vocabulary

base

compound growth

decay factor

exponent

exponential decay

exponential form

exponential growth

growth factor

standard form

Prerequisite Units

Thinking with Mathematical Models (Algebra)

NCTM Principles and Standards 2000

Content Standard: Algebra

Process Standards: Problem Solving, Reasoning and Proof, Communication, Connections, and Representation

Materials

Graphing calculators (preferably with the capacity to display a function as a table)

Chessboards (optional)

Counters, such as pennies, chips, or beans (about 65 per group)

Cups for holding hot liquid (1 per group)

Thermometers (1 per group)

Watches or clock

Materials for growing mold: cake pan, glue, bouillon, gelatin, mold from bread or yogurt, plastic wrap, and rubber band (optional; see the Launch section of Problem 2.3)

Quarter inch grid paper (provided as a blackline master)

Large sheets of paper and markers

Very hot water (for Problem 4.4)

Room thermometer

Mathematics in the Unit

- Recognize and describe situations in which variables grow and decay exponentially.
- Recognize and represent exponential patterns with tables, graphs, and equations.
- Compare and contrast exponential relationships with linear relationships.
- Determine growth factors and decay factors in exponential situations.
- Use tables, graphs, and equations to solve problems involving exponential growth and exponential decay.
- Describe the effects of varying the values of a and b in the equation $y = a(b^x)$ on the graph of that equation.

© Prentice-Hall, Inc.

Connections to Other Units

The ideas in *Growing, Growing, Growing* build on and connect to several big ideas in other Connected Mathematics units.

Big Idea	Prior Work	Future Work
building and analyzing exponential models	looking for graphical or symbolic models that describe a pattern in data *(Thinking with Mathematical Models)*	extending the analysis to include all positive real numbers for the domain *(high school)*
reasoning with and about exponential relationships	reasoning about other relationships, such as connections among attributes of geometric figures *(Covering and Surrounding)*; representing relationships with words, pictures, tables, graphs, and equations *(Variables and Patterns; Moving Straight Ahead)*	using tabular, graphical, and symbolic methods to solve problems that involve exponential functions, such as finding half-life or solving equations of the type $a^x = bx$ *(high school)*
exploring the significance of shapes of graphs and patterns in tables	exploring the significance of shapes of graphs and patterns in tables *(Moving Straight Ahead; Thinking with Mathematical Models)*	exploring the significance of shapes of graphs and patterns in tables *(Frogs, Fleas, and Painted Cubes)*; extending the experiences to include recognition of trigonometric relationships *(high school)*
making sense of the symbols in the expression $y = a(b^x)$	attaching meaning to the symbols in a linear equation of the form $y = mx + b$ *(Moving Straight Ahead; Thinking with Mathematical Models)*	making sense of the symbols in quadratic relationships expressed in expanded or factored form *(Frogs, Fleas, and Painted Cubes)*; reviewing and extending the analysis of exponential and quadratic functions *(high school)*; extending the analysis to include the symbolic expressions of trigonometric functions *(high school)*
exploring rates of growth	recognizing the significance of constant additive growth *(Moving Straight Ahead)*	recognizing the significance of the pattern of change in quadratic relationships *(Frogs, Fleas, and Painted Cubes)*; analyzing variable rates of change in polynomial, exponential, and trigonometric functions *(high school)*
recognizing and describing situations that can be modeled with exponential functions	recognizing and describing situations that can be modeled with linear relationships *(Moving Straight Ahead; Thinking with Mathematical Models)*	recognizing and describing situations that can be modeled with quadratic functions *(Frogs, Fleas, and Painted Cubes)*; extending recognition to trigonometric functions *(high school)*
using exponents	using exponents to express large and small quantities *(Data Around Us)*	appyling rules for exponents *(high school)*

© Prentice-Hall, Inc.

Investigation 1: Exponential Growth

Mathematical and Problem-Solving Goals

■ To gain an intuitive understanding of basic experimental growth patterns

■ To begin to recognize exponential patterns in tables, graphs, and equations

■ To solve problems involving exponential growth

■ To express a number that is the product of identical factors in exponential form and stardard form

Problems in this Investigation

Problem 1.1: Making Ballots *(pages 5–7)*

Problem 1.2: Requesting a Reward *(pages 7–8)*

Problem 1.3: Making a New Offer *(pages 8–9)*

Resource Options for Planning

	Suggested Pacing	Assignment Guide (ACE questions)	Materials for Students	Resources for Teachers
Investigation 1	4 days total	Exercises are in Student Edition, pp. 10–15	■ graphing calculators ■ blank transparencies *	■ overhead graphing calculator * ■ Additional Practice, Investigation 1 (TG, pp. 120–121)
Problem 1.1	1 day	4–9, 12	■ 8 1/2" by 11" scrap paper ■ scissors (1 per group)	■ Transparency 1.1 (TG, p. 97) *
Problem 1.2	1 day	1–3, 10, 13	■ Labsheet 1.2 (1 per student) ■ chessboards ■ counters (about 65 per group)	■ Transparency 1.2 (TG, p. 98) * ■ transparency of Labsheet 1.2 * ■ Labsheet 1.2 BLM (TG, p. 96)
Problem 1.3	2 days	11, 14–16		■ Transparency 1.3 (TG, p. 99) * ■ large sheets of paper and markers
Mathematical Reflections		MR 1–3	■ journal	

* optional materials

© Prentice-Hall, Inc.

Investigation 2: Growth Patterns

Mathematical and Problem-Solving Goals

- To recognize patterns of exponential growth in tables and equations
- To compare and contrast exponential growth to linear growth
- To reason with and solve problems involving exponents and exponential growth
- To determine the growth factor in a given exponential model

Problems in this Investigation

Problem 2.1: Getting Costs in Line *(pages 17–18)*

Problem 2.2: Listening to the Queen *(pages 19–20)*

Problem 2.3: Growing Mold *(pages 20–21)*

Resource Options for Planning

	Suggested Pacing	Assignment Guide (ACE questions)	Materials for Students	Resources for Teachers
Investigation 2	4 days total	Exercises are in Student Edition, pp. 22–29	■ graphing calculators ■ class chart from Investigation 1	■ Additional Practice, Investigation 2 (TG, pp. 122–123) ■ overhead graphing calculator *
Problem 2.1	1 day	2–4, 14	■ blank transparencies *	■ Transparency 2.1 (TG, p. 100) *
Problem 2.2	1 day	1, 5–9, 15, 16		■ Transparency 2.2 (TG, p. 101) *
Problem 2.3	2 days	10–13	■ materials for growing mold *	■ Transparency 2.3 (TG, p. 102) * ■ moldy bread *
Mathematical Reflections		MR 1–5	■ journal	

* optional materials

© Prentice-Hall, Inc.

Lesson Planner

Investigation 3: Growth Factors

Mathematical and Problem-Solving Goals

- To determine growth factors and create representations of an exponential population model given sample population data

- To investigate increases in the value of an asset due to compound growth

- To review and extend understanding of percent

Problems in this Investigation

Problem 3.1: Reproducing Rabbits *(pages 31–33)*

Problem 3.2: Investing for the Future *(pages 34–35)*

Problem 3.3: Making a Difference *(pages 36–37)*

Resource Options for Planning

	Suggested Pacing	Assignment Guide (ACE questions)	Materials for Students	Resources for Teachers
Investigation 3	4 days total	Exercises are in Student Edition, pp. 38–43	■ graphing calculators	■ Additional Practice, Investigation 3 (TG, pp. 124–125) ■ overhead graphing calculator *
Problem 3.1	1 day	1, 2, 15, 16, 18		■ Transparency 3.1 (TG, p. 103) *
Problem 3.2	1 day	3–8	■ blank transparencies *	■ Transparency 3.2A (TG, p. 104) * ■ Transparency 3.2B (TG, p. 105) *
Problem 3.3	2 days	9–14, 17		■ Transparency 3.3A (TG, p. 106) * ■ Transparency 3.3B (TG, p. 107) *
Mathematical Reflections		MR 1–3	■ journal	

* optional materials

© Prentice-Hall, Inc.

Lesson Planner

Investigation 4: Exponential Decay

Mathematical and Problem-Solving Goals

- To recognize patterns of exponential decay in tables, graphs, and equations
- To use knowledge of exponents to write equations for models of exponential decay
- To reason about problems involving exponents and exponential decay
- To describe the effects of varying the values of a and b in the equation $y = a(b^x)$ on the graph of that equation

Problems in this Investigation

Problem 4.1: Making Smaller Ballots *(pages 45–47)*

Problem 4.2: Fighting Fleas *(pages 48–49)*

Problem 4.3: Exploring Exponential Equations *(pages 50–51)*

Problem 4.4: Cooling Water *(pages 51–52)*

Resource Options for Planning

	Suggested Pacing	Assignment Guide (ACE questions)	Materials for Students	Resources for Teachers
Investigation 4	5 days total	Exercises are in Student Edition, pp. 53–59	■ graphing calculators	■ overhead graphing calculator* ■ Additional Practice, Investigation 4 (TG, pp. 126–127)
Problem 4.1	1 day	1, 6, 8	■ quarter-inch grid paper (1 per pair) ■ scissors (1 per pair)	■ Transparency 4.1 (TG, p. 108) * ■ Quarter-inch grid paper BLM (TG, p. 117)
Problem 4.2	1 day	2, 4, 9		■ Transparency 4.2 (TG, p. 109) *
Problem 4.3	1 day	3, 5	■ transparent grids or large sheets of paper * ■ quarter-inch grid paper	■ Transparency 4.3 (TG, p. 110) * ■ Quarter-inch grid paper BLM (TG, p. 117)
Problem 4.4	2 days	7, 10	■ very hot water ■ cups for holding hot liquid (1 per group) ■ thermometers (1 per group) ■ watches or clock	■ Transparency 4.4A (TG, p. 111) * ■ Transparency 4.4B (TG, p. 112) * ■ Transparency 4.4C (TG, p. 113) * ■ thermometer for measuring room temperature
Mathematical Reflections		MR 1–3	■ journal	

* optional materials

© Prentice-Hall, Inc.

Frogs, Fleas, and Painted Cubes

Pacing Options

Investigations and Assessments	Class Time (days)
1 Introduction to Quadratic Relationships (SE, pp. 5–18)	4
Check-Up 1 (TG, pp. 87–88)	1/2
2 Quadratic Expressions (SE, pp. 19–40)	6
Check-Up 2 (TG, p. 89)	1/2
3 Quadratic Patterns of Change (SE, pp. 41–51)	4
4 What is a Quadratic Function? (SE, pp. 52–70)	4
Quiz (TG, pp. 90–92)	1
5 Painted Cubes (SE, pp. 71–84)	4
Looking Back and Looking Ahead: Unit Reflections (SE, pp. 85–87)	1
Self-Assessment (TG, p. 100)	take home
Unit Test (TG, pp. 96–98)	1

Teacher's Guide and Ancillary Resources

Assessment Resources (pp. 85–109)

Blackline Masters (pp. 111–143)

Additional Practice (pp. 145–154)

 Assessment and Additional Practice

Essential Vocabulary

constant term	minimum value
expanded form	parabola
factored form	quadratic
function	expression
like terms	quadratic term
line of symmetry	term
linear term	triangular number
maximum value	

Prerequisite Units

Variables and Patterns (Algebra)

Accentuate the Negative (Number and Operations)

Moving Straight Ahead (Algebra)

Thinking with Mathematical Models (Algebra)

NCTM Principles and Standards 2000

Content Standard: Algebra

Process Standards: Problem Solving, Reasoning and Proof, Communication, Connections, and Representation

Materials

Graphing calculators

Square tiles (optional; about 50 per group)

Base ten thousands blocks (optional; 1 per group)

Centimeter or other unit cubes (in four colors or with colored dot stickers), or sugar cubes and colored markers (as many as are available)

String (optional)

Waxed or transparent paper (optional)

Stopwatch (optional)

Motion detector (optional)

Balls (optional)

Rubik's Cube (optional)

Mathematics in the Unit

■ Develop an awareness of quadratic relationships and how they can be recognized from patterns in tables, graphs, and equations.

■ Describe patterns in tables of quadratic functions and predict subsequent entries.

■ Recognize the characteristic shape of the graph of a quadratic function and identify its line of symmetry, vertex, and intercepts.

■ Detect quadratic relationships from the pattern of differences in tables.

■ Match quadratic equations to patterns in tables and graphs.

■ Develop an understanding of equivalent expressions (two expressions that model the same relationship).

■ Recognize a quadratic function from an equation written as a product of two linear factors or in expanded form as $y = ax^2 + bx + c$.

■ Recognize that the same equation can model more than one situation.

■ Predict from tables, graphs, and equations whether quadratic functions have maximum or minimum values, and find those values.

■ Interpret maximum and minimum points and intercepts in projectile-motion problems.

■ Understand the properties that characterize quadratic relationships by comparing quadratic relationships to linear and cubic relationships.

© Prentice-Hall, Inc.

Connections to Other Units

The ideas in *Frogs, Fleas, and Painted Cubes* build on and connect to several big ideas in other Connected Mathematics units.

Big Idea	Prior Work	Future Work
analyzing quadratic relationships by examining tables, graphs, and equations	analyzing linear and exponential relationships (*Variables and Patterns; Moving Straight Ahead; Thinking with Mathematical Models; Growing, Growing, Growing*)	reviewing and extending the analysis of quadratic relationships, with more emphasis on symbolic methods (*high school*)
comparing characteristics of tables and graphs for quadratic relationships with those for linear and exponential relationships and using those characteristics to make predictions	comparing patterns of change in tables and graphs for linear and exponential relationships (*Thinking with Mathematical Models; Growing, Growing, Growing*)	extending the analysis of patterns of change to other polynomial functions and trigonometric functions (*high school*)
understanding the significance of x- and y-intercepts, maximum and minimum points, and lines of symmetry	understanding the significance of x- and y-intercepts of a linear function (*Moving Straight Ahead*); understanding the significance of the y-intercept in exponential functions (*Growing, Growing, Growing*)	understanding the significance of zeroes in solving equations (*high school*); understanding the significance of maxima and minima in applications (*high school*); using symbolic methods for finding zeroes, maxima, and minima (*high school*); applying the quadratic formula and the formula for the vertex of a parabola (*high school*)
understanding the equivalence of two or more symbolic forms	recognizing equivalent forms of rational numbers (*Bits and Pieces I; Bits and Pieces II*)	using the distributive property and similar properties to write equivalent forms of symbolic expressions (*Say it with Symbols*); factoring, expanding, and simplifying expressions, as appropriate to the particular situation (*high school*)
attaching contextual meaning to equations	attaching contextual meaning to m and b in linear relationships of the form $y = mx + b$ and to a and b in exponential relationships of the form $y = a(b^x)$	attaching contextual meaning to different forms of linear and quadratic relationships (*Say It with Symbols*); attaching contextual meaning to different forms of polynomial and trigonometric functions (*high school*)
informally recognizing that altering the choices for the range or the scale of each axis can alter the shape or view of the graph	understanding the significance of scale in constructing and interpreting graphs from data (*Data About Us, Data Around Us*)	exploring issues of practical and theoretical domain and range (*high school*)

© Prentice-Hall, Inc.

Lesson Planner

Investigation 1: Introduction to Quadratic Relationships

Mathematical and Problem-Solving Goals

- To develop an awareness of quadratic functions and how to recognize them from patterns in tables and graphs

- To describe patterns in tables of quadratic functions and predict subsequent entries

- To recognize the characteristic shape of the graph of a quadratic function and observe such features as lines of symmetry, maximum points, and intercepts

- To use tables and graphs of quadratic relationships to answer questions about a situation

- To represent some quadratic relationships with equations

Problems in this Investigation

Problem 1.1: Staking a Claim *(page 6)*

Problem 1.2: Reading a Graph *(pages 7–9)*

Problem 1.3: Writing an Equation *(pages 10–11)*

Resource Options for Planning

	Suggested Pacing	Assignment Guide (ACE questions)	Materials for Students	Resources for Teachers
Investigation 1	4 days total	Exercises are in Student Edition, pp. 12–17	■ graphing calculators ■ grid paper	■ Additional Practice, Investigation 1 (TG, pp. 146–148) ■ overhead graphing calculator * ■ Grid paper BLM (TG, p. 143)
Problem 1.1	1 day	3, 4, 11	■ string * ■ square tiles (about 50 per group) *	■ Transparency 1.1A (TG, p. 115) * ■ Transparency 1.1B (TG, p. 116) * ■ string * ■ transparent grid * ■ grid paper BLM (TG, p. 143)
Problem 1.2	1 day	5, 7–9		■ Transparency 1.2A (TG, p. 117) * ■ Transparency 1.2B (TG, p. 118) * ■ Transparency 1.2C (TG, p. 119) * ■ Transparency 1.2D (TG, p. 120) *
Problem 1.3	2 days	1, 2, 6, 10, 12		■ Transparency 1.3 (TG, p. 121) *
Mathematical Reflections		MR 1–4	■ journal	

* optional materials

© Prentice-Hall, Inc.

Lesson Planner

Investigation 2: Quadratic Expressions

Mathematical and Problem-Solving Goals

- To develop an awareness of quadratic functions and how they can be recognized from patterns in tables, graphs, and equations

- To recognize a characteristic shape of the graph of a quadratic function and identify its line of symmetry, vertex, and intercepts

- To develop an understanding of equivalent expressions, that is, of two expression that model the same relationship

- To recognize a quadratic function from an equation, written as a product of two linear factors, or in expanded form as $ax^2 + bx + c$

Problems in this Investigation

Problem 2.1: Day 1: Trading Land *(pages 20–21)*

Problem 2.2: Day 2: Changing One Dimension *(pages 22–24)*

Problem 2.3: Day 3: Changing Both Dimensions *(pages 24–27)*

Problem 2.4: Day 4: Looking Back at Parabolas *(pages 28–30)*

Resource Options for Planning

	Suggested Pacing	Assignment Guide (ACE questions)	Materials for Students	Resources for Teachers
Investigation 2	6 days total	Exercises are in Student Edition, pp. 31–39	■ graphing calculators ■ grid paper	■ Additional Practice, Investigation 2 (TG, pp. 148–149) ■ overhead graphing calculator * ■ Grid paper BLM (TG, p. 143)
Problem 2.1	1 day	1, 2, 32, 35		■ transparent grid * ■ blank transparency * ■ Transparency 2.1 (TG, p. 122) *
Problem 2.2	1 day	3, 33, 34, 36		■ Transparency 2.2A (TG, p. 123) * ■ Transparency 2.2B (TG, p. 124) *
Problem 2.3	2 days	4–8, 22–26, 37, 40–43		■ Transparency 2.3A (TG, p. 125) * ■ Transparency 2.3B (TG, p. 126) *
Problem 2.4	2 days	9–21, 27–31, 38, 39, 44–46	■ Labsheet 2.4 (1 per student)	■ Transparency 2.4A (TG, p. 127) * ■ Transparency 2.4B (TG, p. 128) * ■ transparency of Labsheet 2.4 * ■ Labsheet 2.4 BLM (TG, p.112) ■ waxed or transparent paper *
Mathematical Reflections		MR 1–5	■ journal	

* optional materials

© Prentice-Hall, Inc.

Investigation 3: Quadratic Patterns of Change

Mathematical and Problem-Solving Goals

■ To observe and describe patterns of regularity and change in data

■ To express data from a problem situation in tables, graphs, and equations

■ To make predictions based on data

■ To observe the pattern of change in a quadratic relationship and use it to predict the next entry in a table

■ To understand that the same equation may model different situations

Problems in this Investigation

Problem 3.1: Counting Handshakes *(pages 41–43)*

Problem 3.2: Exploring Triangular Numbers *(pages 43–44)*

Resource Options for Planning

	Suggested Pacing	Assignment Guide (ACE questions)	Materials for Students	Resources for Teachers
Investigation 3	4 days total	Exercises are in Student Edition, pp. 45–50	■ graphing calculators ■ grid paper	■ Additional Practice, Investigation 3 (TG, pp. 150–151) ■ overhead graphing calculator * ■ Grid paper BLM (TG, p. 143)
Problem 3.1	2 days	1, 9–13 15, 17		■ Transparency 3.1A (TG, p. 129) * ■ Transparency 3.1B (TG, p. 130) *
Problem 3.2	2 days	2–8, 14, 16, 18, 19		■ Transparency 3.2 (TG, p. 131) *
Mathematical Reflections		MR 1–3	■ journal	

* optional materials

© Prentice-Hall, Inc.

Lesson Planner

Investigation 4: What Is a Quadratic Function?

Mathematical and Problem-Solving Goals

■ To predict from tables, graphs, and equations whether quadratic functions have maximum or minimum values

■ To find and interpret maximum and minimum values from tables, graphs, and the factored form of equations

■ To describe patterns of change in tables and graphs of quadratic relationships

■ To make predictions based on data

Problems in this Investigation

Problem 4.1: Tracking a Ball *(pages 53–55)*

Problem 4.2: Measuring Jumps *(pages 55–57)*

Problem 4.3: Putting It All Together *(pages 57–59)*

Resource Options for Planning

	Suggested Pacing	Assignment Guide (ACE questions)	Materials for Students	Resources for Teachers
Investigation 4	4 days total	Exercises are in Student Edition, pp. 60–69	■ graphing calculator ■ grid paper	■ Additional Practice, Investigation 4 (TG, pp. 152–153) ■ overhead graphing calculator * ■ Grid paper BLM (TG, p. 143)
Problem 4.1	1 day	1, 2, 11–15, 19		■ Transparency 4.1A (TG, p. 132) * ■ balls * ■ stopwatch * ■ motion detector *
Problem 4.2	1 day	3, 9, 16–18, 26–28	■ blanks transparencies *	■ Transparency 4.2A (TG, p. 133) * ■ Transparency 4.2B (TG, p. 134) * ■ Transparency 4.2C (TG, p. 135) *
Problem 4.3	2 days	4–8, 10, 20–25	■ Labsheets 4.3A and 4.3B (1 per student) *	■ Transparency 4.3A (TG, p. 136) * ■ Transparency 4.3B (TG, p. 137) * ■ transparencies of Labsheets 4.3A and 4.3B * ■ Labsheets 4.3A and 4.3B BLM (TE, pp. 113–114) *
Mathematical Reflections		MR 1–4	■ journal	

* optional materials

© Prentice-Hall, Inc.

Investigation 5: Painted Cubes

Mathematical and Problem-Solving Goals

- To observe patterns in tables of data
- To express data from a problem situation in tables, graphs, and equations
- To make predictions based on data
- To develop a deeper sense of the properties that characterize quadratic relationships by comparing quadratic relationships to linear and cubic relationships

Problems in this Investigation

Problem 5.1: Analyzing Cube Puzzles *(pages 71–73)*

Problem 5.2: Exploring Painted-Cube Patterns *(pages 73–74)*

Resource Options for Planning

	Suggested Pacing	Assignment Guide (ACE questions)	Materials for Students	Resources for Teachers
Investigation 5	4 days total	Exercises are in Student Edition, pp. 75–83	■ graphing calculators ■ grid paper ■ base ten thousands blocks (1 per group) * ■ centimeter or other unit cubes (in four colors or with colored stickers) or sugar cubes and colored markers	■ Additional Practice, Investigation 5 (TG, p. 154) ■ Grid paper BLM (TG, p. 143) ■ overhead graphing calculator * ■ Rubik's Cube, base ten thousands block or other large cube *
Problem 5.1	2 days	1, 5, 7–13		■ Transparency 5.1A (TG, p. 138) * ■ Transparency 5.1B (TG, p. 139) *
Problem 5.2	2 days	2–4, 6, 14–25		■ Transparency 5.2 (TG, p. 140) *
Mathematical Reflections		MR 1–3	■ journal	

* optional materials

© Prentice-Hall, Inc.

Unit Organizer

Say It with Symbols

Pacing Options

Investigations and Assessments	Class Time (days)
1 Order of Operations (SE, pp. 5–19)	4
Check-Up 1 (TG, p. 75)	1/2
2 Equivalent Expressions (SE, pp. 20–33)	4
3 Some Important Properties (SE, pp. 34–52)	5
Quiz (TG, pp. 76–77)	1
4 Solving Equations (SE, pp. 53–64)	5
Check-Up 2 (TG, p. 78)	1/2
5 Writing Expressions for Surface Area (SE, pp. 65–70)	2
Looking Back and Looking Ahead: Unit Reflections (SE, pp. 73–75)	1
Self-Assessment (TG, p. 87)	take home
Unit Test (TG, pp. 82–85)	1
Unit Project (SE, pp. 71–72)	1 or 2

Teacher's Guide and Ancillary Resources

Assessment Resources (pp. 73–99)

Blackline Masters (pp. 101–131)

Additional Practice (pp. 133–143)

 Assessment and Additional Practice

Essential Vocabulary

commutative property of addition	expanded form
commutative property of multiplication	factored form
	parabola
distributive property	roots
equivalent expressions	term

Prerequisite Units

Variables and Patterns (Algebra)

Accentuate the Negative (Number and Operations)

Moving Straight Ahead (Algebra)

Thinking with Mathematical Models (Algebra)

Growing, Growing, Growing (Algebra)

Frogs, Fleas, and Painted Cubes (Algebra)

NCTM Principles and Standards 2000

Content Standard: Algebra

Process Standards: Problem Solving, Reasoning and Proof, Communication, Connections, and Representation

Materials

Trapezoids cut from Labsheet 3.3 (optional)

Graphing calculators (preferably with the capacity to display a function as a table)

Square tiles (optional)

Cuisenaire rods (4 to 6 of the same color rod plus 3 or 4 unit rods per pair of students)

Manufactured cubes or sugar cubes (optional, for the Unit Project; ideally at least 60 per student)

Large sheets of paper (at least 1 per pair)

Transparency of Labsheet 3.3 (optional)

Pan balance (optional)

Mathematics in the Unit

- Review and strengthen understanding of the conventional *order of operation* rules in the context of practical problems.

- Evaluate expressions by applying the rules of order of operations.

- Write symbolic sentences that communicate reasoning.

- Develop tools for manipulating symbolic expressions in ways that are both connected to and independent from tabular, graphical, and contextualized reasoning.

- Recognize applications of the distributive and commutative properties.

- Recognize and interpret equivalent expressions.

- Reason about and use equivalent expressions.

- Explain the reasoning behind the solution of linear equations.

- Understand and use symbolic expressions involving addition, subtraction, multiplication, division, and exponents.

- Judge the equivalency of two or more expressions by examining the underlying reasoning and the related tables and graphs.

- Apply the properties for mathematically manipulating expressions to solving linear equations.

- Solve simple quadratic equations demonstrating an understanding of basic factoring and "undoing" techniques.

© Prentice-Hall, Inc.

Connections to Other Units

The ideas in *Say It With Symbols* build on and connect to several big ideas in other Connected Mathematics units.

Big Idea	Prior Work	Future Work
making sense of symbols	making sense of linear, quadratic, exponential, and other symbolic expressions *(Variables and Patterns; Moving Straight Ahead; Thinking with Mathematical Models; Growing, Growing, Growing; Frogs, Fleas, and Painted Cubes)*	making sense of polynomial, logarithmic, trigonometric, and rational symbolic expressions and functions *(high school)*
using the appropriate order of operations in evaluating expressions	evaluating and making sense of symbolic expressions *(Variables and Patterns; Moving Straight Ahead; Thinking with Mathematical Models; Growing, Growing, Growing; Frogs, Fleas, and Painted Cubes)*	evaluating and making sense of polynomial, logarithmic, trigonometric, and rational expressions *(high school)*
writing symbolic sentences, using parentheses and properties of real numbers, to communicate effectively	writing symbolic sentences *(Variables and Patterns; Moving Straight Ahead; Thinking with Mathematical Models; Growing, Growing, Growing; Frogs, Fleas, and Painted Cubes)*	writing equivalent expressions involving polynomial, logarithmic, trigonometric, and rational expressions that communicate reasoning using the properties of real numbers *(high school)*
reasoning with equivalent expressions	reasoning with equivalent expressions *(Bits and Pieces I; Bits and Pieces II; Variables and Patterns; Moving Straight Ahead; Thinking with Mathematical Models; Growing, Growing, Growing; Frogs, Fleas, and Painted Cubes)*	reasoning with equivalent expressions to solve problems that can be modeled by polynomial, logarithmic, trigonometric, and rational functions *(high school)*
solving linear and quadratic equations	solving linear and quadratic equations using tables, graphs, and simple symbolic rules *(Variables and Patterns; Moving Straight Ahead; Thinking with Mathematical Models; Growing, Growing, Growing; Frogs, Fleas, and Painted Cubes)*	developing a deeper understanding of solving linear and quadratic equations and applying and extending the techniques to solving polynomial and rational equations *(high school)*
modeling and solving problems	modeling and solving problems *(Variables and Patterns; Moving Straight Ahead; Thinking with Mathematical Models; Growing, Growing, Growing; Frogs, Fleas, and Painted Cubes)*	modeling and solving problems using polynomial, logarithmic, and trigonometric functions *(high school)*

© Prentice-Hall, Inc.

Lesson Planner

Investigation 1: Order of Operations

Mathematical and Problem-Solving Goals

- To make sense of symbolic expressions involving addition, subtraction, multiplication, division, and exponents

- To develop an understanding of the conventional *order of operations* rules by being attentive to the ways expressions are written and evaluated in a variety of settings

- To evaluate expressions by applying the rules of order of operations

Problems in this Investigation

Problem 1.1: Adding and Multiplying *(pages 5–8)*

Problem 1.2: Dividing *(pages 8–9)*

Problem 1.3: Working with Exponents *(pages 10–11)*

Resource Options for Planning

	Suggested Pacing	Assignment Guide (ACE questions)	Materials for Students	Resources for Teachers
Investigation 1	4 days total	Exercises are in Student Edition, pp. 12–18	■ graphing calculators	■ Additional Practice, Investigation 1 (TG, pp. 134–135) ■ overhead graphing calculator *
Problem 1.1	1 day	1–5, 18–22, 29, 31–33		■ Transparency 1.1 (TG, p. 103) *
Problem 1.2	1 day	23–28, 30		■ Transparency 1.2A (TG, p. 104) * ■ Transparency 1.2B (TG, p. 105) *
Problem 1.3	2 days	6–17, 34–42		■ Transparency 1.3A (TG, p. 106) * ■ Transparency 1.3B (TG, p. 107) *
Mathematical Reflections		MR 1–3	■ journal	

* optional materials

© Prentice-Hall, Inc.

Lesson Planner

Investigation 2: Equivalent Expressions

Mathematical and Problem-Solving Goals

- To informally articulate the distributive property
- To apply the distributive property to simplify and compare expressions
- To further articulate what it means for two expressions to be equivalent
- To judge the equivalency of two or more expressions by examining the reasoning that each represents
- To determine the equivalency of two or more expressions by examining tables and graphs

Problems in this Investigation

Problem 2.1: Tiling Pools *(pages 20–21)*

Problem 2.2: Thinking in Different Ways *(pages 22–23)*

Problem 2.3: Diving In *(pages 23–25)*

Resource Options for Planning

	Suggested Pacing	Assignment Guide (ACE questions)	Materials for Students	Resources for Teachers
Investigation 2	4 days total	Exercises are in Student Edition, pp. 26–32	■ graphing calculators ■ grid paper ■ square tiles *	■ Additional Practice, Investigation 2 (TG, pp. 136–137) ■ overhead graphing calculator * ■ transparent grid * ■ square tiles for overhead * ■ Grid paper BLM (TG, p. 130)
Problem 2.1	1 day	1–3		■ Transparency 2.1 (TG, p. 108) *
Problem 2.2	1 day	19, 23–25	■ large sheets of paper or blank transparencies *	■ Transparency 2.2A (TG, p. 109) * ■ Transparency 2.2B (TG, p. 110) *
Problem 2.3	2 days	4–18, 20–22		■ Transparency 2.3 (TG, p. 111) *
Mathematical Reflections		MR 1–4	■ journal	

* optional materials

© Prentice-Hall, Inc.

Investigation 3: Some Important Properties

Mathematical and Problem-Solving Goals

■ To determine the impact of a negative quantity as a factor

■ To use the distributive and commutative properties to show equivalence of expressions

■ To use contextual clues to interpret symbolic expressions

■ To solve a variety of problems using the distributive and commutative properties

Problems in this Investigation

Problem 3.1: Walking Together *(pages 36–37)*

Problem 3.2: Estimating Profit *(pages 37–39)*

Problem 3.3: Finding the Area of a Trapezoid *(pages 39–40)*

Problem 3.4: Writing Quadratic Expressions *(pages 41–43)*

Resource Options for Planning

	Suggested Pacing	Assignment Guide (ACE questions)	Materials for Students	Resources for Teachers
Investigation 3	5 days total	Exercises are in Student Edition, pp. 44–51	■ graphing calculators	■ Additional Practice, Investigation 3 (TG, pp. 138–140) ■ overhead graphing calculator *
Problem 3.1	1 day	2, 4, 11, 12, 19–21, 38, 48–51		■ Transparency 3.1A (TG, p. 112) * ■ Transparency 3.1B (TG, p. 113) *
Problem 3.2	1 day	1, 3, 5–10, 25–29, 46, 47		■ Transparency 3.2A (TG, p. 114) * ■ Transparency 3.2B (TG, p. 115) * ■ Transparency 3.2C (TG, p. 116) *
Problem 3.3	1 day	13–18, 22–24 39–42, 52–57	■ trapezoids cut from Labsheet 3.3 * ■ large sheets of paper *	■ Transparency 3.3 (TG, p. 117) * ■ transparency of Labsheet 3.3 * ■ Labsheet 3.3 BLM (TG, p. 102)
Problem 3.4 **Mathematical Reflections**	2 days	30–37, 43–45 MR 1, 2	■ large sheets of paper or blank transparencies * ■ journal	■ Transparency 3.4A (TG, p. 118) * ■ Transparency 3.4B (TG, p. 119) *

* optional materials

© Prentice-Hall, Inc.

Investigation 4: Solving Equations

Mathematical and Problem-Solving Goals

- To apply the properties for manipulating expressions to solving linear equations
- To solve simple quadratic equations symbolically
- To connect the solutions of an equation to information about its table and graph

Problems in this Investigation

Problem 4.1: Comparing Costs *(pages 53–54)*

Problem 4.2: Solving Linear Equations *(pages 54–55)*

Problem 4.3: Reasoning with Symbols *(page 56)*

Problem 4.4: Solving Quadratic Equations *(pages 57–58)*

Resource Options for Planning

	Suggested Pacing	Assignment Guide (ACE questions)	Materials for Students	Resources for Teachers
Investigation 4	5 days total	Exercises are in Student Edition, pp. 59–63	■ graphing calculators ■ grid paper * ■ blank transparencies * ■ transparent grids *	■ Additional Practice, Investigation 4 (TG, pp. 141–142) ■ overhead graphing calculator * ■ transparent grid * ■ Grid paper BLM (TG, p. 130) *
Problem 4.1	1 day	5, 16		■ Transparency 4.1 (TG, p. 120) *
Problem 4.2	1 day	1, 2, 11	■ large sheets of paper *	■ Transparency 4.2A (TG, p. 121) * ■ Transparency 4.2B (TG, p. 122) * ■ pan balance *
Problem 4.3	1 day	3, 4, 12, 13, 20, 21		■ Transparency 4.3 (TG, p. 123) *
Problem 4.4	2 days	6–10, 14, 15, 17–19, 22–27		■ Transparency 4.4A (TG, p. 124) * ■ Transparency 4.4B (TG, p. 125) * ■ Transparency 4.4C (TG, p. 126) *
Mathematical Reflections		MR 1–3	■ journal	

* optional materials

© Prentice-Hall, Inc.

Investigation 5: Writing Expressions for Surface Area

Mathematical and Problem-Solving Goals

- To find and compare equivalent expressions in a given context
- To evaluate expressions for a specific value of a variable

Problems in this Investigation

Problem 5.1: Stacking Rods *(pages 65–66)*

Resource Options for Planning				
	Suggested Pacing	**Assignment Guide** (ACE questions)	**Materials for Students**	**Resources for Teachers**
Investigation 5	2 days total	Exercises are in Student Edition, pp. 67–69	■ graphing calculators ■ Cuisenaire rods (4 to 6 of the same color rod plus 3 or 4 unit rods per pair of students) ■ centimeter rulers * ■ large sheets of paper (1 per pair)	■ Additional Practice, Investigation 5 (TG, p. 143) ■ overhead graphing calculator * ■ Cuisenaire rods for the overhead projector *
Problem 5.1	2 days	1–6		■ Transparency 5.1 (TG, p. 127) *
Mathematical Reflections		MR 1, 2	■ journal	

* optional materials

© Prentice-Hall, Inc.

Unit Organizer

Kaleidoscopes, Hubcaps, and Mirrors

Pacing Options

Investigations and Assessments	Class Time (days)
1 Three Types of Symmetry (SE, pp. 5–23)	4
Check-Up 1 (TG, p. 79)	1/2
2 Symmetry Transformations (SE, pp. 24–41)	6
Quiz (TG, pp. 80–83)	1
3 Transforming Coordinates (SE, pp. 42–58)	6
Check-Up 2 (TG, pp. 84–85)	1/2
4 Symmetry and Algebra (SE, pp. 59–70)	4
Looking Back and Looking Ahead: Unit Reflections (SE, pp. 76–77)	1
Self-Assessment (TG, p. 95)	take home
Unit Test (TG, pp. 90–93)	1
Unit Project (SE, pp. 110–113, optional)	take home

Teacher's Guide and Ancillary Resources

Assessment Resources (pp. 77–113)

Blackline Masters (pp. 115–181)

Additional Practice (pp. 183–195)

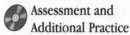 Assessment and Additional Practice

Essential Vocabulary

congruent figures	symmetry
line reflection	transformation
reflectional symmetry	translation
rotation	translational
rotational symmetry	symmetry

Prerequisite Units

Shapes and Designs (Geometry, Measurement)

NCTM Principles and Standards 2000

Content Standard: Geometry

Process Standards: Problem Solving, Reasoning and Proof, Communication, Connections, and Representation

Materials

Paper copies of triangle *ABC*, square *ABCD*, and hexagon *ABCDEF* (cut from the blackline masters)

Graphing calculators

Transparent reflection tools (such as Image Reflectors™)

Mirrors

Angle rulers or protractors (1 per student)

Compasses (1 per student)

Tracing paper (or lightweight plain paper)

Centimeter and quarter-inch grid paper

1-inch-wide paper strips

Transparencies of Labsheets 1.ACE1, 1.ACE2, 1.ACE3, 1.ACE4, 2.1B, 2.2, 2.3B, 2.4B, 2.ACE1, 2.ACE2, 2.ACE3, 2.ACE4, 4.1A, 4.1B, 4.2A, 4.2B, and 4.ACE (optional)

Computer graphics software (optional; for demonstration)

Rubber stamp (optional)

Chalkboard compass (optional)

Mathematics in the Unit

- Understand important properties of symmetry.
- Recognize and describe symmetries of figures.
- Use tools to examine symmetries and transformations.
- Create figures with specified symmetries.
- Identify basic design elements that can be used to replicate a given design.
- Perform symmetry transformations of figures, including reflections, translations, and rotations.
- Give precise mathematical directions for performing reflections, rotations, and translations.
- Write coordinate rules for specifying the image of a general point (x, y) under particular transformations.
- Combine transformations and find a single transformation that will produce the same result.
- Find the symmetries of geometric figures and make tables showing the results of combining symmetry transformations.
- Learn to appreciate the power of transformational geometry to describe motions, patterns, and designs in the real world.

© Prentice-Hall, Inc.

Connections to Other Units

The ideas in *Kaleidoscopes, Hubcaps, and Mirrors* build on and connect to several big ideas in other Connected Mathematics units.

Big Idea	Prior Work	Future Work
recognizing symmetry in designs; determining the design element that has been reflected, rotated, or translated to produce a design with symmetry; creating designs with reflectional, rotational, or translational symmetries	recognizing and completing mirror reflections (*Shapes and Designs; Ruins of Montarek*); recognizing and completing designs with rotational symmetry (*Shapes and Designs*); rotating cube buildings (*Ruins of Montarek*); recognizing, analyzing, and producing tessellations (*Shapes and Designs*)	recognizing symmetry in graphs of functions (*high school*); applying the ideas of symmetry to other subjects, such as graphic design and architecture (*high school and college*)
looking for patterns that can be used to predict attributes of designs	looking for regularity and using patterns to make predictions (*all Connected Mathematics units*)	making inferences and predictions based on observation and proving predictions (*high school and college*)
relating rigid motions to the concept of symmetry	relating similarity transformations to the concept of similarity (*Stretching and Shrinking*)	describing symmetry in graphs, such as graphs of quadratic functions, periodic functions, and power functions (*high school*)
describing rigid motions in words and with coordinate rules	describing similarity transformations in words and with coordinate rules (*Stretching and Shrinking*)	using matrices to represent transformations (*high school*)
composing symmetry transformations	performing similarity transformations (*Stretching and Shrinking*)	composing functions; recognizing graphs of certain functions as transformations of graphs of other functions, such as recognizing that the graph of $f(x) = (x + 2)^2$ is the graph of $f(x) = x^2$ shifted 2 units to the left (*high school*)
making tables of combinations of symmetry transformations for geometric figures and exploring the group structure in the tables	making tables for real-number operations (*elementary school*); looking at the properties of real-number operations (*Say It with Symbols*)	studying the algebraic structure of groups, rings, and fields (*high school and college*)

© Prentice-Hall, Inc.

Investigation 1: Three Types of Symmetry

Mathematical and Problem-Solving Goals

- To explore reflectional, rotational, and translational symmetry informally
- To explore the use of tools, such as tracing paper, to analyze designs to determine their symmetries
- To design shapes that have specified symmetries
- To identify basic design elements that can be used to replicate a design

Problems in this Investigation

Problem 1.1: Reflectional Symmetry *(pages 6–7)*

Problem 1.2: Rotational Symmetry *(pages 8–9)*

Problem 1.3: Symmetry in Kaleidoscope Designs *(pages 10–11)*

Problem 1.4: Translational Symmetry *(pages 12–14)*

Resource Options for Planning

	Suggested Pacing	Assignment Guide (ACE questions)	Materials for Students	Resources for Teachers
Investigation 1	4 days total	Exercises are in Student Edition, pp. 15–22	■ graphing calculators ■ tracing paper ■ rulers ■ mirrors ■ transparent reflection tools such as Image Reflectors	■ overhead graphing calculator * ■ Additional Practice, Investigation 1 (TG, pp. 184–185)
Problem 1.1	1 day	4–7, 18a-18e	■ Labsheet 1.1 (1 per student) ■ Labsheet 1. ACE2 (1 per student) ■ tracing paper ■ compasses (1 per student)	■ Transparency 1.1 (TG, p. 147) * ■ Labsheet 1.1 BLM (TG, p. 116) ■ transparency of Labsheet 1. ACE2* ■ Labsheet 1. ACE2 BLM (TG, p. 121)
Problem 1.2	1 day	1–3, 13–17, 18f, 18g	■ Labsheet 1.2 (1 per student) ■ angle rulers or protractors ■ Labsheet 1. ACE1 (1 per student) ■ tracing paper ■ compasses	■ Transparency 1.2A (TG, p. 148) * ■ Transparency 1.2B (TG, p. 149) * ■ Labsheet 1.2 BLM (TG, p. 117) ■ transparency of Labsheet 1. ACE1* ■ Labsheet 1. ACE1 BLM (TG, p. 120)
Problem 1.3	1 day	25–33	■ Labsheet 1.3 (1 per student) ■ markers ■ angle rulers or protractors	■ Labsheet 1.3 BLM (TG, p. 118) ■ Transparency 1.3 (TG, p. 150) * ■ two mirrors *
Problem 1.4	1 day	8–12, 19–24	■ Labsheet 1.4 (1 per student) ■ Labsheets 1. ACE2, 1. ACE3, 1. ACE4, (1 each per student) ■ markers ■ angle rulers or protractors ■ 1-inch-wide paper strips ■ tracing paper ■ compasses ■ blank transparencies *	■ Transparency 1.4 (TG, p. 151) * ■ transparencies of Labsheets 1. ACE2, 1. ACE3, 1. ACE4 * ■ Labsheet 1.4 BLM (TG, p. 119) ■ Labsheets 1. ACE2, 1. ACE3, 1. ACE4 BLM (TG, pp. 121–123) ■ rubber stamp *
Mathematical Reflections		MR 1, 2	■ journal	

* optional materials

© Prentice-Hall, Inc.

Lesson Planner

Investigation 2: Symmetry Transformations

Mathematical and Problem-Solving Goals

- To examine reflections, translations, and rotations to determine how to specify such transformations precisely

- To use the properties of reflections, translations, and rotations to perform transformations

- To find lines of reflection, magnitudes and directions of translations, and centers and angles of rotation

- To examine the results of combining reflections over two intersecting lines or two parallel lines, two translations, or two rotations to find a single transformation that will produce the same result

Problems in this Investigation

Problem 2.1: Describing Line Reflections *(pages 24–27)*   Problem 2.3: Describing Rotations *(pages 29–31)*

Problem 2.2: Describing Translations *(pages 27–29)*   Problem 2.4: Combining Transformations *(pages 32–33)*

Resource Options for Planning

	Suggested Pacing	Assignment Guide (ACE questions)	Materials for Students	Resources for Teachers
Investigation 2	6 days total	Exercises are in Student Edition, pp. 34–40	■ graphing calculators ■ tracing paper ■ rulers ■ angle rulers or protractors ■ compasses ■ mirrors ■ transparent reflection tools	■ Additional Practice, Investigation 2 (TG, pp. 186–189) ■ overhead graphing calculator * ■ transparent ruler * ■ chalkboard compass * ■ blank transparencies
Problem 2.1	1 day	1–4, 9, 19	■ Labsheets 2.1A, 2.1B, 2.ACE1, 2.ACE3 (1 each per student)	■ Transparencies 2.1A, 2.1B (TG, pp. 152–153) * ■ transparencies of Labsheets 2.1B, 2.ACE1, 2.ACE3 * ■ Labsheets 2.1A, 2.1B, 2.ACE1, 2.ACE3 BLM (TG, pp. 124, 125, 131,133)
Problem 2.2	1 day	5, 6, 11, 17	■ Labsheets 2.2, 2.ACE2, 2.ACE3 (1 each per student)	■ Transparencies 2.2A, 2.2B (TG, pp. 154–155) * ■ transparencies of Labsheet 2.2, 2.ACE2, 2.ACE3 * ■ Labsheets 2.2, 2.ACE2, 2.ACE3 BLM (TG, p. 126, 132, 133)
Problem 2.3	2 days	7, 8, 10, 16, 18, 20	■ Labsheets 2.3A, 2.3B, 2.ACE2, 2.ACE3 (1 each per student) ■ blank transparencies	■ Transparencies 2.3A, 2.3B, (TG, pp. 156–157) * ■ transparencies of Labsheets 2.3B, 2.ACE2, 2.ACE3 * ■ Labsheets 2.3A, 2.3B, 2.ACE2, 2.ACE3 BLM (TG, pp. 127, 128, 132, 133)
Problem 2.4	2 days	12–15, 21–23	■ Labsheets 2.4A, 2.4B, 2.ACE4 (1 each per student)	■ Transparencies 2.4A, 2.4B (TG, pp. 158–159) * ■ transparencies of Labsheet 2.4B, 2.ACE4 * ■ Labsheets 2.4A, 2.4B, 2.ACE4 BLM (TG, pp. 129, 130, 134)
Mathematical Reflections		MR 1–5	■ journal	

* optional materials

© Prentice-Hall, Inc.

Lesson Planner

Investigation 3: Transforming Coordinates

Mathematical and Problem-Solving Goals

- To write directions for drawing figures composed of line segments
- To analyze the vertices of a figure under a transformation and to specify translations with coordinate rules
- To recognize that a transformation of the form $(x, y) \rightarrow (x + a, y + b)$ is a translation of point (x, y) a units in the x direction and b units in the y direction
- To specify rotations of 90°, 180°, 270°, and 360° with coordinate rules
- To specify reflections over the x-axis, the y-axis, and the line $y = x$
- To combine transformations to find single, equivalent transformations
- To understand the relationship between symmetry transformations and congruence

Problems in this Investigation

Problem 3.1: Writing Rules for Reflections *(pages 42–44)*

Problem 3.2: Writing Rules for Translations *(pages 45–47)*

Problem 3.3: Writing Rules for Rotations *(pages 47–48)*

Problem 3.4: Relating Symmetry to Congruence *(pages 48–49)*

Resource Options for Planning

	Suggested Pacing	Assignment Guide (ACE questions)	Materials for Students	Resources for Teachers
Investigation 3	6 days total	Exercises are in Student Edition, pp. 50–57	■ graphing calculators ■ centimeter or quarter-inch grid paper	■ Additional Practice, Investigation 3 (TG, pp. 190–193) ■ overhead graphing calculator * ■ centimeter or quarter-inch grid paper BLM (TG, pp. 179–180)
Problem 3.1	1 day	1–3, 9–11, 15	■ Labsheets 3.1A, 3.1B (1 each per group) * ■ tracing paper ■ Labsheet 3.ACE1 (1 per student)	■ Transparencies 3.1A, 3.1B, 3.1C (TG pp. 160–162) * ■ Labsheets 3.1A, 3.1B, 3.ACE1 BLM (TG, pp. 135,136, 139) ■ computer graphics software * ■ transparent centimeter grid *
Problem 3.2	1 day	6–8, 17, 19–21		■ Transparencies 3.2A, 3.2B, 3.2C, 3.2D (TG, pp. 163–166) *
Problem 3.3	2 days	4, 12–14, 18, 22–24	■ Labsheet 3.3 (1 per group) ■ tracing paper ■ Labsheet 3.ACE2 (1 per student)	■ Transparencies 3.3A, 3.3B (TG, pp. 167–168) * ■ transparent centimeter grid * ■ Labsheets 3.3, 3.ACE2 BLM (TG, pp. 137, 140)
Problem 3.4	2 days	5, 16, 25–27	■ Labsheets 3.4, 3.ACE3 (1 each per student) ■ rulers (1 per student) ■ angle rulers or protractors (1 per student)	■ Transparency 3.4 (TG, p. 169) ■ Labsheets 3.4, 3.ACE3 BLM (TG, pp. 138, 141) ■ transparent ruler *
Mathematical Reflections		MR 1–10	■ journal	

* optional materials

© Prentice-Hall, Inc.

Lesson Planner

Investigation 4: Symmetry and Algebra

Mathematical and Problem-Solving Goals

- To determine the possible symmetry transformations for a given polygon

- To construct a table showing all possible results of combining two symmetry transformations of a given polygon

- To analyze such a table to determine whether (1) there is an identity element for the "and then" operation, (2) each element has an inverse for the "and then" operation, and (3) the "and then" operation is commutative

Problems in this Investigation

Problem 4.1: Transforming Triangles *(pages 60–61)*
Problem 4.2: Transforming Squares *(pages 61–62)*
Problem 4.3: Properties of the Combining Operation *(pages 62–63)*

Resource Options for Planning

	Suggested Pacing	Assignment Guide (ACE questions)	Materials for Students	Resources for Teachers
Investigation 4	4 days total	Exercises are in Student Edition, pp. 64–69	■ graphing calculators	■ overhead graphing calculator* ■ Additional Practice, Investigation 4 (TG, pp. 194–195)
Problem 4.1	1 day	7, 8	■ paper copies of triangle *ABC* (1 per student) ■ Labsheeets 4.1A and 4.1B (1 each per student) ■ Labsheet 4.ACE (1 per student)	■ Transparency 4.1 (TG, p. 170) * ■ Labsheeets 4.1A and 4.1B BLM (TG, pp. 142–143) ■ transparency of Labsheet 4.ACE * ■ Labsheet 4.ACE BLM (TG, p. 146)
Problem 4.2	1 day	1a, 1b, 2a, 2b, 3a, 3b, 6, 11a, 11b	■ paper copies of square *ABCD* (1 per student) ■ Labsheeets 4.2A and 4.2B (1 each per student)	■ Transparency 4.2 (TG, p. 171) * ■ Labsheeets 4.2A and 4.2B BLM (TG, pp. 144–145)
Problem 4.3 **Mathematical Reflections**	2 days	1c–e, 2c–e, 3c–e, 4, 5, 9, 10, 11c–e, 12, 13 MR 1–3	■ journal	■ Transparency 4.3A (TG, p. 172) * ■ Transparency 4.3B (TG, p. 173) *

* optional materials

© Prentice-Hall, Inc.

Samples and Populations

Pacing Options

Investigations and Assessments	Class Time (days)
1 Comparing Data Sets (SE, pp. 5–23)	5
Check-Up (TG, pp. 69–70)	1/2
2 Conducting Surveys (SE, pp. 24–36)	4
3 Random Samples (SE, pp. 37–48)	4
Quiz (TG, pp. 71–72)	1
4 Solving Real-World Problems (SE, pp. 49–62)	3
Looking Back and Looking Ahead: Unit Reflections (SE, pp. 67–69)	1
Self-Assessment (TG, p. 80)	take home
Unit Test or Unit Project (TG, pp. 76–78 or SE, pp. 63–66)	1 or 2

Teacher's Guide and Ancillary Resources

Assessment Resources (pp. 67–93)

Blackline Masters (pp. 95–127)

Additional Practice (pp. 129–140)

 Assessment and Additional Practice

Essential Vocabulary

biased sample	representative sample
box-and-whiskers plot (box plot)	sample
convenience sample	scatter plot
distribution	stem-and-leaf plot (stem plot)
five-number summary	
histogram	systematic sample
population	voluntary-response sample
random sample	

Prerequisite Units

Data About Us (Data Analysis and Probability)

NCTM Principles and Standards 2000

Content Standard: Data Analysis and Probability

Process Standards: Problem Solving, Reasoning and Proof, Communication, Connections, and Representation

Materials

Graphing calculators

Statistical computer software, such as Statistics Workshop (see TG, p. 10)

10-section spinners (provided as BLM)

12-section spinners (provided as BLM)

10-sided number cubes

Paper clips or bobby pins

Overhead graphing calculator (optional)

Two brands of peanut butter, crackers, and two knives for spreading (optional)

Large sheets of paper

Mathematics in the Unit

■ Employ statistical investigation to explore problems.

■ Analyze data using tables, stem-and-leaf plots, histograms, and box-and-whiskers plots.

■ Compare data using measures of center (mean, median), measure of spread (range, percentiles), and data displays (stem-and-leaf plots, box-and-whiskers plots).

■ Explore relationships among data using scatter plots.

■ Distinguish between samples and populations, compare samples, and use information drawn from samples to make conclusions about populations.

■ Apply selected concepts from probability to understand the concept of randomness and to select random samples.

■ Explore concepts of representativeness and sample size as they relate to using random and nonrandom samples to draw conclusions about the characteristics of populations.

■ Design a survey, focusing on how questions are asked.

© Prentice-Hall, Inc.

Connections to Other Units

The ideas in *Samples and Populations* build on and connect to several big ideas in other Connected Mathematics units.

Big Idea	Prior Work	Future Work
using the process of statistical investigation to explore problems	beginning to use the process of statistical investigation (*Data About Us*)	continue to frame exploration of statistical concepts within the process of statistical investigation (*high school*)
composing and decomposing graphs and recognizing the elements of graphs, the interrelationships among graphical elements, and the impact of these elements on the presentation of information in a graph	working with a variety of graphs, including line plots, bar graphs, circle graphs, stem-and-leaf plots, histograms, box-and-whiskers plots, and scatter plots (*elementary grades, Data About Us, Bits and Pieces II*)	reviewing and extending work with graphs to emphasize scatter plots and line graphs that consider such relationships as change over time (*high school*)
describing the shape of the data in a graph, including such elements as clusters, gaps, outliers, symmetry or skew, what is typical, the spread in the data, and single or multiple peaks in the data	working with a variety of data contexts involving problems that are meaningful to students and discussing what is known once data are collected and represented (*elementary grades, Data About Us, Data Around Us*)	reviewing and extending work with graphs, particularly extending measures of spread to include the concept of standard deviation (*high school*)
distinguishing between a sample and a population; raising questions about the representativeness of sample data and sources of bias; and using different ways to generate samples, paying special attention to random sampling	informally exploring concepts as part of the process of statistical investigation in applied situations (*elementary grades, Data About Us, How Likely Is It?, What Do You Expect?*)	placing greater emphasis on using and selecting samples and ways to address representativeness and bias (*high school*)

© Prentice-Hall, Inc.

Lesson Planner

Investigation 1: Comparing Data Sets

Mathematical and Problem-Solving Goals

■ To engage in the process of statistical investigation

■ To compare data using tables, stem-and-leaf plots, histograms, and box-and-whiskers plots

■ To compare data using measures of center (mean and median) and measures of spread (range)

■ To consider the properties of the mean and the median, particularly the influence of extreme values on each measure's calculation

Problems in this Investigation

Problem 1.1: Comparing Quality Ratings *(page 7)*
Problem 1.2: Using Box-and-Whiskers Plots *(pages 7–10)*
Problem 1.3: Comparing Prices *(pages 10–11)*
Problem 1.3: Making a Quality Choice *(page 12)*
Problem 1.3: Comparing Quality and Price *(pages 12–14)*

Resource Options for Planning

	Suggested Pacing	Assignment Guide (ACE questions)	Materials for Students	Resources for Teachers
Investigation 1	5 days total	Exercises are in Student Edition, pp. 15–22	■ graphing calculators ■ computers and statistical software * ■ grid paper	■ Additional Practice, Investigation 1 (TG, pp. 130–135) ■ overhead graphing calculator * ■ grid paper BLM (TG, p. 125)
Problem 1.1	1 day	5, 7	■ Labsheet 1.1 (1 per student) *	■ Transparency 1.1A (TG, p. 103) * ■ Transparency 1.1B (TG, p. 104) * ■ Transparency 1.1C (TG, p. 105) * ■ Labsheet 1.1 BLM (TG, p. 96) ■ two brands of peanut butter * ■ crackers * ■ two knives *
Problem 1.2	1 day	6		■ Transparency 1.2A (TG, p. 106) * ■ Transparency 1.2B (TG, p. 107) *
Problem 1.3	1 day	8		■ Transparency 1.3A (TG, p. 108) * ■ Transparency 1.3B (TG, p. 109) *
Problem 1.4	1 day	1, 3	■ blank transparencies	■ Transparency 1.4 (TG, p. 110) *
Problem 1.5	1 day	2, 4, 9	■ Labsheet 1.ACE (1 per student) *	■ Transparency 1.5 (TG, p. 109) * ■ Labsheet 1.ACE BLM (TG, p. 97)
Mathematical Reflections		MR 1–4	■ journal	

* optional materials

© Prentice-Hall, Inc.

Investigation 2: Conducting Surveys

Mathematical and Problem-Solving Goals

- To distinguish between a sample and a population
- To consider various ways of developing a sampling plan
- To use data from a sample to make predicitons about a population
- To design a survey, focusing on how questions are asked

Problems in this Investigation

Problem 2.1: Asking About Honesty *(pages 25–26)*
Problem 2.2: Selecting a Sample *(pages 26–28)*
Problem 2.3: Asking the Right Questions *(pages 29–30)*

Resource Options for Planning

	Suggested Pacing	Assignment Guide (ACE questions)	Materials for Students	Resources for Teachers
Investigation 2	4 days total	Exercises are in Student Edition, pp. 31–35	■ graphing calculators ■ computers and statistical software * ■ grid paper	■ Additional Practice, Investigation 2 (TG, p. 136) ■ overhead graphing calculator * ■ grid paper BLM (TG, p. 125)
Problem 2.1	1 day	1–4		■ Transparency 2.1 (TG, p. 116) *
Problem 2.2	1 day	5–11		■ Transparency 2.2 (TG, p. 117) * ■ large sheets of paper *
Problem 2.3 **Mathematical Reflections**	2 days	12–15 MR 1–3	■ blank transparencies or large sheets of paper * ■ journal	■ Transparency 2.3 (TG, p. 118) *

* optional materials

© Prentice-Hall, Inc.

Lesson Planner

Investigation 3: Random Samples

Mathematical and Problem-Solving Goals

- To select a random sample from a population
- To use sampling distributions, measures of center, and measures of spread to describe and compare samples
- To use data from samples to estimate a characteristic of a population
- To apply elementary probability work with spinners or calculators to choosing random samples of data

Problems in this Investigation

Problem 3.1: Choosing Randomly *(page 37)*
Problem 3.2: Selecting a Random Sample *(pages 38–40)*
Problem 3.3: Choosing a Sample Size *(pages 41–42)*

Resource Options for Planning

	Suggested Pacing	Assignment Guide (ACE questions)	Materials for Students	Resources for Teachers
Investigation 3	4 days total	Exercises are in Student Edition, pp. 43–47	■ graphing calculators ■ computers and statistical software * ■ grid paper	■ Additional Practice, Investigation 3 (TG, pp. 137–138) ■ overhead graphing calculator * ■ grid paper BLM (TG, p. 125)
Problem 3.1	1 day	7, 8		■ Transparency 3.1 (TG, p. 116 *)
Problem 3.2	1 day	9	■ Labsheet 3.2A (1 per group) ■ Labsheet 3.2B and/or transparencies of Labsheet 3.2B (2 per group) * ■ 10-section spinners ■ 10-sided number cubes ■ paper clips or bobby pins	■ Transparency 3.2 (TG, p. 117) * ■ transparency of Labsheet 3.2B * ■ Labsheets 3.2A and 3.2B BLM (TG, pp. 98–99) ■ 10-section spinners BLM (TG, p. 126)
Problem 3.3	2 days	1–6, 10, 11	■ Labsheet 3.3 (1 per student) * ■ spinners and number cubes from Problem 3.2 *	■ Transparency 3.3A (TG, p. 118) * ■ Transparency 3.3B (TG, p. 119) * ■ Transparency 3.3C (TG, p. 120) * ■ transparency of Labsheet 3.3 * ■ Labsheet 3.3 BLM (TG, p. 100)
Mathematical Reflections		MR 1–5	■ journal	

* optional materials

© Prentice-Hall, Inc.

Investigation 4: Solving Real-World Problems

Mathematical and Problem-Solving Goals

- To use data from samples to estimate a characteristic found in a population
- To use characteristics from a population to describe a sample
- To apply elementary probability in choosing random samples of data

Problems in this Investigation

Problem 4.1: Solving an Archaeological Mystery *(pages 49–52)*

Problem 4.2: Simulating Cookies *(pages 52–54)*

Resource Options for Planning

	Suggested Pacing	Assignment Guide (ACE questions)	Materials for Students	Resources for Teachers
Investigation 4	3 days total	Exercises are in Student Edition, pp. 55–61	■ graphing calculators ■ computers and statistical software * ■ grid paper	■ Additional Practice, Investigation 4 (TG, pp. 139–140) ■ overhead graphing calculator * ■ grid paper BLM (TG, p. 125)
Problem 4.1	1 day	1, 4, 5, 7–11		■ Transparency 4.1 (TG, p. 124) *
Problem 4.2	2 days	2, 3, 6, 12, 13	■ 12-section spinners * ■ blank transparencies *	■ Transparency 4.2 (TG, p. 125) * ■ 12-section spinners BLM (TG, p. 127)
Mathematical Reflections		MR 1–3	■ journal	

* optional materials

© Prentice-Hall, Inc.

Unit Organizer

Clever Counting

Pacing Options

Investigations and Assessments	Class Time (days)
1 Counting Possibilities (SE, pp. 5–14)	3
2 Opening Locks (SE, pp. 15–26)	4
Check-Up (TG, pp. 60–61)	1/2
3 Networks (SE, pp. 27–36)	3
4 Deciding Whether Order Is Important (SE, pp. 37–46)	3
Quiz (TG, pp. 62–63)	1
5 Wrapping Things Up (SE, pp. 47–56)	2
Looking Back and Looking Ahead: Unit Reflections (SE, pp. 59–61)	1
Self-Assessment (TG, p. 71)	take home
Unit Test (TG, pp. 67–69)	1
Unit Project (SE, pp. 57–58, optional)	1

Teacher's Guide and Ancillary Resources

Assessment Resources (pp. 59–81)

Blackline Masters (pp. 83–100)

Additional Practice (pp. 101–109)

 Assessment and Additional Practice

Essential Vocabulary

counting tree

edge

network

node

Prerequisite Units

None

NCTM Principles and Standards 2000

Content Standard: Number and Operations, Data Analysis and Probability

Process Standards: Problem Solving, Reasoning and Proof, Communication, Connections, and Representation

Materials

Graphing calculators

Large sheets of paper

Cuisenaire rods (optional)

Overhead display model of students' graphing calculators (optional)

Combination lock (optional)

Set of dominoes or set of overhead dominoes (provided as BLM)

Mathematics in the Unit

- Recognize situations in which counting techniques apply.
- Construct organized lists of outcomes for complex processes and uncover patterns that help in counting the outcomes of those processes.
- Analyze using counting trees.
- Use mental arithmetic to make estimates in multiplication and division calculations.
- Invent strategies for solving problems that involve counting.
- Analyze counting problems involving choices in various contexts.
- Differentiate among situations in which order does and does not matter and in which repetition is and is not allowed.
- Analyze the number of paths in a network.
- Compare the structures of networks with problems involving combinations.
- Create networks that satisfy given conditions.
- Apply thinking and reasoning skills to an open-ended situation in which assumptions must be made, and create a persuasive argument to support a conjecture.

© Prentice-Hall, Inc.

Connections to Other Units

The ideas in *Clever Counting* build on and connect to several big ideas in other
Connected Mathematics units.

Big Idea	Prior Work	Future Work
understanding and comparing large numbers	scaling quantities and objects up and down; comparing quantities expressed as decimals, percents, and fractions; and comparing categorical and numerical data (*Data About Us; Bits and Pieces II; Comparing and Scaling; Filling and Wrapping; Data Around Us*)	continuing the study of counting, graph theory, and probability (*high school*)
constructing organized lists and counting trees to enumerate possibilities	listing all possible outcomes (*How Likely Is It? What Do You Expect?*); finding all the rectangles and prisms that fit given constraints (*Covering and Surrounding; Filling and Wrapping*); making factor trees to find prime factorizations (*Prime Time*)	continuing the study of counting, graph theory, and probability (*high school*); continuing the study of number theory (*high school*)
recognizing patterns, generalizing patterns, and using patterns to make predictions	looking for regularity and making predictions (virtually every unit provides these opportunities; the algebra units are especially rich: *Variables and Patterns; Moving Straight Ahead; Thinking with Mathematical Models; Looking for Pythagoras; Growing, Growing, Growing; Frogs, Fleas, and Painted Cubes; Say It with Symbols*)	making inferences and predictions based on observing patterns and proving the existence of patterns (*high school and beyond*)
recognizing situations that call for multiplication or division	developing algorithms for performing calculations with fractions, decimals, and percents (*Bits and Pieces I; Bits and Pieces II*); applying knowledge of ratio, proportion, and percent (*Comparing and Scaling*); understanding the multiplicative structure of numbers (*Prime Time; Covering and Surrounding: Filling and Wrapping; Data Around Us*)	continuing the study of counting, graph theory, and probability (*high school*); continuing the study of number theory (*high school*)
inventing and using the fundamental counting principle	understanding the multiplicative structure of numbers (*Prime Time; Covering and Surrounding: Filling and Wrapping; Data Around Us*)	continuing the study of counting, graph theory, and probability (*high school*); continuing the study of number theory (*high school*)

© Prentice-Hall, Inc.

Investigation 1: Counting Possibilities

Mathematical and Problem-Solving Goals

- To analyze counting problems involving choices in different contexts
- To analyze the usefulness of counting trees
- To use counting trees
- To begin to see a connection between some counting situations and the operation of multiplication

Problems in this Investigation

Problem 1.1: Making Faces *(pages 6–7)*

Problem 1.2: Checking Plate Numbers *(page 8)*

Resource Options for Planning				
	Suggested Pacing	**Assignment Guide** (ACE questions)	**Materials for Students**	**Resources for Teachers**
Investigation 1	3 days total	Exercises are in Student Edition, pp. 9–13	■ graphing calculators	■ Additional Practice, Investigation 1 (TG, pp. 134–135)
Problem 1.1	1 day	1, 2, 4, 5, 13, 14	■ large sheets of paper *	■ Transparency 1.1 (TG, p. 85) *
Problem 1.2	2 days	3, 6–12, 15–19		■ Transparency 1.2 (TG, p. 86) * ■ license plate *
Mathematical Reflections		MR 1–3	■ journal	

* optional materials

© Prentice-Hall, Inc.

Lesson Planner

Investigation 2: Opening Locks

Mathematical and Problem-Solving Goals

- To further explore counting situations in which multiplication provides an answer
- To construct systematic lists of outcomes for complex processes
- To uncover patterns that help in counting the outcomes of complex processes
- To recognize that one problem has the same structure as another problem

Problems in this Investigation

Problem 2.1: Pushing Buttons *(pages 15–16)*
Problem 2.2: Dialing Combinations *(pages 16–17)*
Problem 2.3: Increasing Security *(pages 18–19)*

Resource Options for Planning

	Suggested Pacing	Assignment Guide (ACE questions)	Materials for Students	Resources for Teachers
Investigation 2	4 days total	Exercises are in Student Edition, pp. 20–25	■ graphing calculators	■ Additional Practice, Investigation 2 (TG, pp. 136–137)
Problem 2.1	1 day	1, 8–10		■ Transparency 2.1 (TG, p. 87) *
Problem 2.2	1 day	2–4, 11, 14		■ Transparency 2.2 (TG, p. 88) * ■ combination lock *
Problem 2.3	2 days	5–7, 12, 13		■ Transparency 2.3 (TG, p. 89) *
Mathematical Reflections		MR 1–4	■ journal	

* optional materials

© Prentice-Hall, Inc.

Lesson Planner

Investigation 3: Networks

Mathematical and Problem-Solving Goals

- To explore network applications
- To analyze the number of paths in a network
- To compare the structures of networks and problems involving combinations
- To create networks that satisfy given constraints

Problems in this Investigation

Problem 3.1: Making Rounds *(pages 27–28)*

Problem 3.2: Networking *(pages 28–29)*

Problem 3.3: Designing Networks *(pages 30–31)*

Resource Options for Planning

	Suggested Pacing	Assignment Guide (ACE questions)	Materials for Students	Resources for Teachers
Investigation 3	3 days total	Exercises are in Student Edition, pp. 32–35	■ graphing calculators	■ Additional Practice, Investigation 3 (TG, pp. 138–140) ■ overhead graphing calculator *
Problem 3.1	1 day	1		■ Transparency 3.1A (TG, p. 90) * ■ Transparency 3.1B (TG, p. 91) *
Problem 3.2	1 day	3, 4, 9, 10	■ large sheets of paper *	■ Transparency 3.2 (TG, p. 92) *
Problem 3.3	1 day	2, 5–8		■ Transparency 3.3A (TG, p. 93) * ■ Transparency 3.3B (TG, p. 94) *
Mathematical Reflections		MR 1–3	■ journal	

* optional materials

© Prentice-Hall, Inc.

Investigation 4: Deciding Whether Order Is Important

Mathematical and Problem-Solving Goals

- To identify the difference in the structure of problems in which order is not important from those in which it is

- To create a model to clarify a situation

- To generalize a pattern

Problems in this Investigation

Problem 4.1: Playing Dominoes *(pages 37–38)*

Problem 4.2: Choosing Locks *(pages 39–40)*

Resource Options for Planning

	Suggested Pacing	Assignment Guide (ACE questions)	Materials for Students	Resources for Teachers
Investigation 4	3 days total	Exercises are in Student Edition, pp. 41–45	■ graphing calculators	■ Additional Practice, Investigation 4 (TG, pp. 141–142)
Problem 4.1	1 day	1, 2, 5, 9–13		■ Transparency 4.1A (TG, p. 95) * ■ Transparency 4.1B (TG, p. 96) * ■ set of dominoes or set of overhead dominoes (BLM; TG, p. 95)
Problem 4.2	2 days	3, 4, 6–8, 14		■ Transparency 4.2 (TG, p. 97) *
Mathematical Reflections		MR 1, 2	■ journal	

* optional materials

© Prentice-Hall, Inc.

Investigation 5: Wrapping Things Up

Mathematical and Problem-Solving Goals

- To recognize situations in which counting techniques apply

- To differentiate among situations in which order does and does not matter and in which repetition is and is not allowed

- To use a variety of models to clarify a solution

- To consider situations in which counting techniques would not apply

- To apply thinking and reasoning skills to an open-ended situation in which assumptions must be made, and to create a persuasive argument to support a conjecture

Problems in this Investigation

Problem 5.1: Catching a Bicycle Thief *(pages 47–49)*

Resource Options for Planning				
	Suggested Pacing	**Assignment Guide** (ACE questions)	**Materials for Students**	**Resources for Teachers**
Investigation 5	2 days total	Exercises are in Student Edition, pp. 50–55	■ graphing calculators	■ Additional Practice, Investigation 5 (TG, p. 143)
Problem 5.1	2 days	1–17		■ Transparency 5.1 (TG, p. 98) *
Mathematical Reflections		MR 1–4	■ journal	

* optional materials

© Prentice-Hall, Inc.